Adam's Eve

A Handbook for the Social Revolution-
ECOA and the Story of Adam and Eve ©

Jon C. Hall, J.D. and Barbara D. Hall

Bloomington, IN  Milton Keynes, UK

AuthorHouse™
1663 Liberty Drive, Suite 200
Bloomington, IN 47403
www.authorhouse.com
Phone: 1-800-839-8640

AuthorHouse™ UK Ltd.
500 Avebury Boulevard
Central Milton Keynes, MK9 2BE
www.authorhouse.co.uk
Phone: 08001974150

© 2007 Jon C. Hall, J.D. and Barbara D. Hall. All rights reserved.

No part of this book may be reproduced, stored in a retrieval system, or transmitted by any means without the written permission of the author.

First published by AuthorHouse 6/14/2007

ISBN: 978-1-4259-2060-9 (sc)

Printed in the United States of America
Bloomington, Indiana

This book is printed on acid-free paper.

This book is dedicated to tomorrow's children,
lest we forget that what we do today will
determine the world in which they are born and
the culture in which they will live.

ACKNOWLEDGEMENTS

This book would not have been possible without those people, both men and women, who chose to remain anonymous, but who willingly shared incidents in their personal lives in the hopes that others would be spared from a similar fate.

I would like to personally thank my sister Barbara D. Hall who encouraged me to take a fresh look at my Adam and Eve speeches to the Florida banking industry and planted the seeds for the preliminary ideas for this work. In addition, I appreciate greatly the encouragement from Glory Read to undertake this project and whose editorial comments were most important. Again, much appreciation and thanks go to my sister, whose untiring efforts and support in being a sounding board assisted in making this book a reality both in the ideas and assistance in writing this manuscript. Without her continued support and belief in my abilities, this book would not have been possible. Her continued guidance, perspective, and editorial assistance in the preparation of the preliminary and rewriting the final drafts were crucial for the completion of this book.

I would like to commend my brother Jon C. Hall for his untiring persistence in working on the preliminary drafts. His ability to ingest and synthesize a vast amount of information contributed to the organization of the material and information for *Adam's Eve*. Also, the creation of two critical works of social research by Susan Faludi who wrote **STIFFED** and **BACKLASH**, provided the backbone of information on the status of the American male and female in society today. I am honored to have finished writing and editing the final manuscript for publication.

I thank my father, Russell S. Hall for his unwavering support for both Jon and I in the preliminary, middle stages and final preparation of this book, including long hours of telephone and personal discussions. Thanks go to Ed Charlton for fine-tuning my ideas for the cover design. And without question, thanks go to the continued support of The Write Group in Montclair, New Jersey.

    Jon C. Hall , J.D.   Barbara D. Hall

INTRODUCTION

For our enlightened and advanced society, it is a sad commentary that a high percentage of marriages have failed since the mid 1960's. Even more disconcerting are the studies that show many women whose marriages survived this tumultuous period insist that if they could start their lives over again, they would chose a different person as their spouse. There are even some scholars who go so far as to predict the end of marriage. These experts overlook the fact we have experienced a social revolution. There is another explanation for the reaction of married women in these studies.

What the experts have overlooked is that women have been changed by the social revolution. Looking back at who they were when they spoke their wedding vows, they would barely recognize themselves when compared to who they are today. In fact, many react the way they do today because they no longer think and act the way they did before the revolution. On the other side of the sexual divide, many husbands remain mired in the traditions of the past.

No one can deny that the social revolution has altered our society forever. To survive in today's world, we must understand how we have been changed by the revolution. To prosper, we need to learn how to avoid the dangers both to property and personal relations that arise due to the unconscious influences of old habits and traditions that are increasingly out of date, but tenaciously embedded in our psyche.

Jon C. Hall , J.D.   Barbara D. Hall

PROLOGUE

Listen my children and you shall hear
A fairy tale from both far and near

Told by a bard of the Village called Lime,
Back in a year well before our time

He spoke of a maiden both young and fair,
A pauper princess, her prospects quite bare,

Barefoot, in rags, an orphan as well
A servant girl to the lord of the dell.

She worked and worked, her morale quite low,
At night the poor princess had nowhere to go.

Her future seemed especially bleak
Her life she thought was past its peak

One night she saw upon the Innhouse stair
A handsome young prince. Could he really be there?

Please, she thought, don't go away.
And back he came the very next day.

A knight was he in shiny bright armor,
Her eyes did glow, amour, amour.

In time he came and called her by name.
The sound to her was just like fame.

He swept her up upon his loyal steed,
Off to his castle at the top of the mead

I'll provide and protect you for the rest of your life.
Marry me now and be my wife.

Forever and more, my handsome young prince.
Forever and more, he spoke with nary a wince.

                              Jon C. Hall, J.D.

TABLE OF CONTENTS

Dedication v
Acknowledgements vii
Introduction... ix
Prologue xi

Chapter One: The Primary Images 1
Chapter Two: Historical Foundation 7
Chapter Three: A New Point Of View 17
Chapter Four: The Great Divide 23
Chapter Five: Credit Clash With Culture........................ 41
Chapter Six: Property Ownership.................................. 63
Chapter Seven: Individual Ownership 73
Chapter Eight: Tenants In Common............................... 85
Chapter Nine: Joint Tenancy 95
Chapter Ten: Special Situations 103
Chapter Eleven: Dangerous Assumptions.....................115
Chapter Twelve: Parties To The Transaction 123
Chapter Thirteen: A Matter Of Trust........................... 143
Chapter Fourteen: Castles In The Sand 155
Chapter Fifteen: Light At The End Of The Tunnel 171
Chapter Sixteen: A Reality Check 179
Chapter Seventeen: New Culture Dreams 203
Chapter Eighteen: Living Today 209

Epilogue 215
About The Authors...219

CHAPTER ONE: THE PRIMARY IMAGES

Many say that the most important asset a person has in this world is their name. Yet, in our society, the one thing a woman gives up in the marriage ceremony is her name. The individual marriage partners start the wedding day as James T. Rowe and Mary Jane Smith. Yet, at the end of the day, when they pull away from the curb in the limousine on their way to the reception, they are transformed to James T. Rowe and Mary Rowe, his wife, also known as Mrs. James T. Rowe. While there are a few women who defy this tradition and retain their maiden names, by far, the vast majority of women willingly accept this process of transformation as an integral part of the wedding ritual, without question.

In today's world where personal identity is so important, some brave individuals are beginning to question why we follow this practice. Yet, no one can deny this tradition continues, generation after generation. The question remains, where did this custom originate, and why do we follow it without question? Why does the father of the bride give the bride away in the marriage ceremony and not the mother?

Our premise for this book is that marriage customs are an expression of the internal self-perceptions that control our lives. Two unconscious but interrelated images act as a template for our behavior. Within these internalized images, we can find the answer for why we continue to celebrate the marriage ceremony the way we do.

The first of these images consists of the story of the creation of Eve. In the old biblical fable, Eve came into being by the tearing out of part of poor Adam's rib. This story of the creation of Eve describes her, not as an equal, but as subordinate to Adam in that she was created from part of him. Nevertheless, the story was adopted long ago as the cornerstone of our culture.

However, the story needed to be moderated to repair the trauma of such a violent act. This violent, unsettling aspect of the creation of Eve was made acceptable by the adoption of marriage as the celebration of the merger of the female, represented by Eve, back into the male, represented by Adam. Thus, the violence of the act of Eve's creation was softened by marriage, making poor Adam whole again. This combined story has become subconsciously interwoven into the core of our culture and has contributed to why women give up their names.

While we have internalized this picture of the marriage ceremony as the celebration of the merger of Eve back into Adam whereby the modern Eve, Mary Jane Smith, becomes Mrs. James T. Rowe. The adoption of this practice began long ago and led to many ramifications for women that reach far beyond the innocent appearance of her name change. In making poor Adam whole again, we have adopted habits that turn Eve into a non-entity to the extent she is reduced to nothing more than *Adam's Eve*, belonging to and a part of Adam. The woman's separate identity is lost forever, overshadowed by her husband.

In fact, the old fable story became so entwined into the very fabric of our society that it influences most of our social structures today. In light of the many changes in society since our forefathers first landed on our shores, this may seem a bit surprising. However, there is a reason many behaviors from the past remain with us even today. That reason is culture.

To understand why culture is the binding force that keeps old practices with us, it helps to review exactly what is meant by the word *culture*. The applicable definition in Webster's New Collegiate Dictionary defines culture as follows:

> The integrated pattern of human behavior that includes thought, speech, action, and artifacts and depends upon man's capacity for learning and transmitting knowledge to succeeding generations.

This standard dictionary definition limits the description of culture to outward observable expressions. To dramatize the premise that the unseen force that binds us to traditions of the past is culture, we have expanded the definition:

> Culture consists of internalized pictures that make up our self-perception. Common traits such as dress, speech, physical

characteristics, and social actions that are passed, without thought, from generation to generation are expressions of these images.

An archaeologist studying the human past looks for pieces of ancient pottery. Ancient pottery has proven to be a good outward expression of culture of the period. Pottery in ancient times was marked exactly the same way for centuries. Over time, a characteristic pattern was adopted as an integral part of a culture and was transferred without thought from generation to generation. While the standardized inscription of pottery as a means of group identification is a practice mostly limited to cultures of long ago, we still identify ourselves by language, dress, social conduct, and other common but observable characteristics. There is a problem with making culture the source of the power that binds us to practices of long ago. When attempting to visualize culture, nothing appears other than a few of the outward observable manifestations.

Easily, culture can be identified by the things we do automatically, without thought as in the dictionary definition. More challenging are the observations and studies of behavior and things done unconsciously. In addition, culture acts both within ourselves, as well as from without and through the influence of others. The important point here is that culture is not limited to any race, creed, national origin, sex, or age. Instead, culture is all-pervasive and can be found within everyone living today.

The story of Eve and the ceremony that symbolically repairs the violence of her creation is a part of how we define ourselves and is one of the two core elements of our culture. Hopefully, we will learn the danger in that this old story induces us to act automatically without thinking. Often the subconscious messages lure us into taking action that may not be in our best interests in the world of reality. To avoid being drawn into bad decisions, we need to develop the practice of stopping long enough to ask questions before making important decisions in our lives.

The second image that defines our culture comes out of the folklore of the Middle Ages. In this picture, we visualize the relationship between males and females by adopting a fantasy image of the old myth of knights and fair maidens. This Middle Age tale tells of a great knight, dressed in shining armor, with lance and shield, wandering on his loyal stead over the countryside. Finally he sees her, a poor maiden, sweeping the steps of a local inn. The knight lifts her up on his gallant horse, and they ride off into the sunset to his castle to live happily ever after. On the way, they come upon the local village nestled in the shadow of the knight's castle seen at the top of a steep hill. High on the parapets of the castle, flags wave in a gentle breeze as he nods proudly in their direction. She smiles in approval as they start on their journey. In this image, the knight will spend his life jousting in tournaments during the week and defending the village on the weekends. In the meantime, the fair maiden waves to him with her handkerchief from high on the battlements of the castle, wishing him well as she awaits his safe return.

Both men and women in our culture carry the combination of this image of the knight and fair maiden mixed with the merger of the female [Eve] back into the male [Adam] to repair the trauma of her creation in our subconscious. These fantastic images are so strong they automatically control the pattern of behavior that we follow throughout our lives. The turmoil men feel today comes from an unconscious lack of motivation or desire to reject these images, especially that of the knight. Within these myths, men see an idealized self-image and lifestyle. The following list provides some of the specific images men see in the knight:

> The knight is in control of his life.
> The knight is lord and master of his realm, including his wife and family.
> The knight is involved with the world outside the castle but from a distance and on his terms.
> The knight has a clear sense of his own importance and purpose.
> The knight is respected as a father.
> The knight is respected as a husband.
> His father, the unseen king who rules over all the castles in the kingdom, respects the knight.
> The knight is able to support and protect his family.
> The knight has lifetime financial security.
> The knight is self-sufficient and stands alone. He does not need anyone else's help, including that of his princess.
> The knight and his castle are a clear part of the bigger kingdom.
> The knight is the idealized symbol of masculinity.
> The knight is confident and free of fear.

For all of the above reasons, most men have no motivation to change the image in their minds in spite of the fact their lives increasingly do not live up to the stereotyped behavior pattern. However, rather than change the image, many men cling to it desperately trying to live in accordance with the rigid conduct inspired by the internal pictures.

Men feel pressure in today's world because masculinity centers on the issue of the inability to provide for the family. Some statistics show American households where men are the sole financial provider may have dropped to as low as eight percent. The old picture of masculinity with the internal perception of men as the knight is no longer representative of today's environment where males exist. However, the image is so enticing that most men unconsciously choose to face the struggle rather than abandon the comfortable perception of being the knight in shining armor.

Women are not immune to the same delusions. They are also caught in the same culture trap. The old image of themselves as fair maidens, coupled with the romantic fantasy of the knight in shining armor who comes to save them, are buried deeply within the subconscious. Yet, women have a different dilemma than men. While the image remains strong, women also see both the failure of men to live up to the image of the knight and, at the same time, they see the possibility of a world beyond a limited life in the castle. This real potential holds far more promise for many women than living in accord with the old behavior pattern. Both of these observations motivate many women to reject the rigid constraints of the old culture images and seek a better life beyond mere existence in the castle. Thus, women are far more likely to change their behavior patterns and, thereby, their lives, than men who remain locked in the old fantasy of the knight. For men, there is a more personal internalized issue relating to their definition of masculinity.

However, women are unconsciously torn by the old images, finding it difficult to give up the image of being the fair maiden. Women are attracted to the image of the fair maiden and her knight for the following reasons:

The maiden is rescued from a life of poverty.
The image offers a life of security for themselves and their children.
They see the knight as sexually loyal.
They see the knight and castle as providing protection.
They see the knight as honorable and trustworthy.
They see the knight as someone who will understand and respond to their feelings and needs.
The knight fits her ideal of masculinity and what a man should be.

Both men and women see something else in this Twelfth Century image that is mutually appealing. In the image, the castle is always high on a hill well above the day-to-day struggle of the people in the village. This element of being above and detached from the problems of everyday life is extremely appealing. Also, the most important part of both images of Adam and Eve and the knight and his fair maiden is that they are simple, clear, and unambiguous. What makes these images doubly alluring is that they are free of any compromise; totally unlike the reality of living in the world we face today. For all these reasons, these old images continue to have a strong hold on us. Like any aspect of culture, they remain buried deep within our subconscious, resistant to change.

Although the core element of culture is the way people think, our premise is that culture is much more than mere thoughts. Both internalized pictures make up culture and outward behavior influences the way the individual thinks. Thus, the internalized images make up the nucleus of culture because they control both behavior and thoughts. The uniform behavior pattern dictated by culture is easily illustrated by the simple comment of the aborigine father to his son. The son presents his father with a piece of pottery where the son used a new pattern created on his own:

> *"That's very nice son. It's very original but we just don't do things that way in our tribe."*

Our internalized pictures set how we define ourselves, including our goals, aspirations, dreams, objectives, and sense of self-worth. After visiting a foreign country, we do not rush home, throw out our wardrobe and start dressing like the people living in the country we visited. The power that keeps our dress and conduct consistent is culture. Culture is such an important part of our lives because we are social beings, and we must live in social groups to survive. We could not live more than a few days without tap water, electricity, gasoline, or food from the grocery store. All these necessities are provided to us by our culture. We can live only in our social group. That glue that holds the group together is culture.

We may fantasize about living on a deserted island when overstressed, but in reality, stark isolation is the one thing we cannot endure. Instead, all we need is a few days vacation with all the modern conveniences of a fancy resort. The boastful claim that we seek an escape from our culture to a deserted island is merely an illusion.

The key to improving the ability to survive in the world today is the development of an increased level of awareness of the power of these pictures to influence our personal thoughts and actions. Increased awareness is the only way to avoid being caught by the imminent dangers to finances, property and personal relationships. Frequently, the unaware act unconsciously following the influence of these old images that lie deeply ingrained in the subconscious.

CHAPTER TWO: HISTORICAL FOUNDATION

We live in a society in crisis. Everyone we talk to, every television show, radio program, newspaper and all the other media tell us we are in a great struggle. We are inundated with descriptions of a war where men blame women and women blame men, with the struggle defined as a battle of gender. While such an explanation is commonly accepted by the public, it does not stand up to close scrutiny. Not only do men blame women as the cause of the crisis, a sizable number of women join in blaming other assertive women. At the same time, a significant percentage of men join women and point to other controlling and prejudicial men for the plight of females.

Fortunately, some individuals look at their spouses and do not see the enemy in the one they love. If we are in a gender war, they ask, why is it so many people are in the wrong camp? The more observant individuals realize the enemy exists because they can feel the stress, anxiety, and tension just like everyone else. They see the force that represses them only as an elusive and invisible enemy. Wisely, they reject the idea that there are two great armies on opposite sides of the field of distrust, each poised to attack blaming the other for their problems. The picture of a gender war where, at the end of each day, each army goes home to cohabit with the other is absurd. To these more discerning individuals, the popular label for the *war* does not fit.

While it is easy to describe the conflict as one where the antagonist is culture, the more pressing issue is why we face such a struggle at all, especially if culture is designed to protect the species for long-range survival. The answer is that culture is slow in changing and lags far behind the rapid changes in the every day reality in which we must survive.

To understand why life today is so different from the imagined internalized images of our culture, we need to be aware that we have just gone through the most significant revolution in this country since the Civil War. To understand what we mean by a revolution we need to define the term. Webster's New Collegiate Dictionary defines a revolution as follows:

> An activity or movement designed to effect fundamental changes in the socioeconomic situation.

What has happened in this country certainly fits that definition. The dictionary does not include it, but when we usually think of a revolution, we think in terms of violent change that happens in a relatively short period of time. The key to any revolution is not violence but that there is a dramatic change in the way a significant percentage of the population thinks, bringing significant, noticeable changes to the entire society. To survive in the world today, we must be aware of the changes our social revolution brought with it. Also, we need to realize that to a large degree, we remain trapped in the customs of the past that are yet unchanged by the revolution.

Most revolutions are portrayed in history books as taking place between fairly precise dates. However, the violence and armed resistance we usually associate with revolutionary events are not evidenced in the social revolution. For this reason, the true beginning and ending dates are harder to identify. Then too, this revolution is fought mostly in the home, behind closed doors, so many of the events and casualties will forever be unknown. Only a few high profile incidents have hinted at the more profound social changes of the revolution as it swept across our country. The beginning and ending dates of the revolution can be determined only by an analysis of more subtle characteristics.

Back in 1965 the number of females in professional degree programs in our colleges and universities was nominal, making up a maximum of three percent of total enrollment. In fact, up until that time, female participation had always been at a one to three percent level. Disinterest of females in the professions had been characteristic of the majority of females since the founding of our country. Back before the revolution, young women went to college with the primary objective of finding a husband. This was a serious and essential undertaking for females because most young women simply had no alternative for economic survival once they graduated from college. However, beginning in 1966 the enrollment of females in career programs began to increase dramatically. More importantly, women in this country changed their life objectives from husband hunting to the development of a professional career. That change in the way they thought was simply revolutionary.

The pre-revolutionary forces that actually started the process of change began many years ago. After all, the first women's rights convention was held back in the year 1848. However, we estimate the year 1966 as the starting date of the revolution. Until then, there was no meaningful permanent social change that affected the lives of women. There were no headlines in the media back in 1966 to announce that the revolution was underway. Most Americans, like those who controlled the media, were totally oblivious to what was happening at the time. We'll never know how many men faced the culture shock when told that the wedding had to be postponed indefinitely so the young women could go on to college and graduate school to advance her career opportunities. Many young men saw only personal rejection, oblivious to the fact they were witnessing the beginning of the social revolution.

If those young women had been a few years older, such decisions would have been unthinkable. Most people realized something was happening, but all they could do was marvel at the change in the enrollment of females in professional career programs. They were unaware of the significance of these decisions to the future of our entire society.

To understand the revolution, we need to understand the forces that led to it. The real foundation for the beginning of the revolution goes back to the Civil War. Before then, somewhere between ninety to ninety five percent of the population of this country lived on small subsistence farms. Life in America was so restrictive that most people never traveled further than a few miles from the place where they were born. This geographical limitation was an important reason people had low personal expectations. Besides, subsistence farming was hard work and involved long hours of routine labor, so there was very little time to think of anything else.

Realistically, there were few other alternatives for males than repeated daily farm drudgery, knowing that, only in time, would they replace their fathers as owners and managers of the farm. The division of labor on the farm automatically placed the male as the head of household. Farm life was demanding and physical brawn was a very real factor in determining who performed specific tasks. In those days, women were more than happy to yield the heavy manual labor to their husbands, brothers, fathers, and sons allowing development of a fairly clear division of labor by gender.

Another factor that led to the revolution was the magical thing we call love. If we can accept the premise that people may possibly fall in love with one in every so many hundred members of the opposite sex they meet, then we can hypothesize that back when our lives were restricted to the farm, there were fewer opportunities to fall in love. No one knows where the magic we call love originated. Love may basically be a bio-chemical reaction that occurs between certain people, and the more people the individual meets the more frequently the individual may fall in love.

Before the Civil War, a good many people in this country lived in a rural environment. Travel was so limited that they probably didn't have the opportunity to fall in love more than once in a lifetime. This simple fact reinforced the myth that, for the individual, there was only one true love in this world. The result was that once people found that first love, generally speaking, they did not look any further. For them, their expectations had been realized. Back in those days, people accepted their first love interest at face value, regardless of the reality of the relationship.

The Civil War changed the horizons for men, taking them out of their narrow lives and exposed them to a larger world beyond the farm. The Civil War also stimulated the adoption of truly interchangeable parts in the manufacturing environment. The one-of-a-kind manufacturing techniques of the early industrial revolution and crude early efforts at mass production evolved into the modern day assembly line. The economic impact of these changes caused population movement into the cities where workers could earn an income that could compete with subsistence living on the farm. Thus, the Civil War served as a major factor for he first significant migration of the population from the farm to the city. This process continues even to this day where the percentage of farmers has dropped to a little more than five percent of our total population.

In the Civil War days, a small percentage of women thought of themselves as individual human beings equal to men. However, the vast majority of women subordinated themselves to men with their role in life limited to that of homemaker. Life in the cities slowly changed these views causing a brief revolutionary moment when women stood up for the right to vote. Once achieved, they went back to the familiar behavior pattern that dated back to the days of life on the farm.

The Second World War was the next significant factor leading to the revolution. Women were needed to take over the jobs men left behind to go to war. A second major movement to the cities took place as industry required a larger wartime work force to meet production demands. During the war years, women became exposed to a life beyond the home. Even though the wartime jobs were often routine, they were still more exciting and stimulating in marked contrast to the drudgery of a life of the homemaker. Women also found satisfaction in earning a wage, and they liked the sense of being a part of the economic world and achievement that it brought to them. For the first time, many women experienced a personal freedom they had not known before. At the same time, women also began to realize that the old concept of a "one and only one" love was not necessarily true. Suddenly, they were exposed to other possibilities.

All these factors raised the expectancy level of women. When men returned home from the war and reclaimed their peacetime jobs, the female work force was sent home. However, they kept the lingering memory of a life beyond a limited domestic existence. Men settled into positions in the new retooled manufacturing base. This change in the work environment led to the creation of our consumer based society, replacing the war machine. At the same time, women were temporarily distracted by the move out to the new suburbs and the flood of new labor saving devices that made their lives as homemakers less monotonous and freed up time for other activities. In fact, for a few brief years, the ideal of the American dream seemed to have come true.

However, the post war euphoria did not last long. In spite of all the fancy new gadgets, more fundamental problems began to surface. One of the cornerstones of life in the home for most women was its promise of security. This promise overpowered feelings of boredom and lack of challenge, but that sense of security began to evaporate as men slowly found themselves unable to maintain a level of income sufficient to provide for their families. Several factors were involved in the demise of the male as sole breadwinner, all of which were beyond the American male's ability to control. Unfortunately, men were not alone; these forces affected both men and their families.

The first of these factors was the government simply did not need the wartime manufacturing capacity any longer to produce high volumes of military equipment and supplies. A process of downsizing military production began that continues even today. Secondly, the crisis nature of the war had inflated the value of the trained laborer. Without that wartime emergency, the jobs that survived simply did not have the economic value they had during the war. As a result, many jobs were adjusted down to a lower market value. These changes not only had a devastating affect on the male employee who needed to support his family, but downsizing had a rippling affect on the whole community. When a large manufacturing plant closed, the businessmen and professionals including doctors, lawyers, dentists, merchants, and others in the community who depended on the local labor force for their income base of the factory workers suffered as well.

The third factor that affected the male's ability to earn a wage sufficient to support his family was the rapid and extensive automation of a large percentage of the skilled assembly line jobs. Thousands of jobs simply disappeared as the economics of assembly by robotic device took over many manual and often highly skilled assembly line and manufacturing operations. Computerization of those robotic devices has accelerated this process even today.

The fourth factor that affected the American male was increased population growth in the third world. This ever-expanding population provided a never-ending source of cheap labor available outside this country. Manufacturing jobs moved to the third world in droves. The relocation of assembly plants and related management and support jobs overseas moved hundreds of thousands more jobs out of this country. Since the third world population continues to expand, the process of the outward flow of manufacturing and related jobs continues with no sign of slowing.

The net effect of all these factors is that many of the jobs created initially by the wartime assembly line have disappeared forever as American workforce jobs. As a result, men have had to learn to accept lower paying jobs when they were lucky enough to secure full time employment. Men simply could not maintain the standard of living that they and their families had learned to expect after the war ended. In addition to these factors, the change in types of jobs available in the country moved to a more service oriented consumer society. The types of jobs that have become available are more low-paying office, retail, and support jobs and fewer high paying skilled positions.

Married women stepped into the workplace to grab the new service jobs to supplement the family income in an attempt to maintain the life style they had grown accustomed after the war. Yet, as this country moved from the 1950's to the 1960's, women comprised no more than a small percentage of the total workforce. However, women jumped at the employment opportunities that were increasingly available, laying the foundation for the revolution.

By the year 1966, the social barrier to the concept of the working woman had disappeared. Since the early 1970's, women have made tremendous gains in obtaining employment in the business world. That movement by women from the home to the workplace is the core of the revolution. Today, more women are working outside the home than at any time in the history of this country. Statistics offer figures that show by the year 2000, women made up 50% of the total workforce, an increase from the 1960's that can only be described as revolutionary. The manifestation of this change was visibly seen by the replacement of the miniskirt by pants suits in women's dress in a few brief years.

In addition, women in the revolution were no longer satisfied with temporary service jobs. They began seeking, not just a college education away from the old home economics courses, but advanced degrees to ensure work in specific professions. The rapidity of this change in thinking is unprecedented in history. Women are now working in middle management positions in our large corporations, and if we can believe the statistics, more women today are starting up new businesses of their own than are men. The change in female employment is indicative of the elevation of women's personal expectations and goals in life. The explosive increase of women in mainstream economic life in this country is a fact, and it has changed our society in a way that is, again, nothing short of revolutionary.

In spite of the advancement of women into mainstream economic life, there are many instances where we still live in a society based on discrimination against women. Many people still believe a woman's place is in the home. These people overlook the fact the revolution has taken place, and, like it or not, it has brought significant changes that are here to stay. These people also fail to recognize that the very concept of the home as limited to husband, wife and biological children has also changed. If women elected to return to the home and abandon their careers today, they would find the memories of the home of the 1960's has changed. Going back to the home they remember and grew up in is no longer an option.

Back in the late 1950's and early 1960's, while some women went to work to help support the family, others reacted in a different way to their husband's inability to provide for the family. They simply packed up and left home, never to return. Divorce, which carried a strong negative social stigma and was a rare event in the 1950's, became a real factor in American life of the 60's. Many of the women of the late 1950s and early 1960's decided their future lay outside their existing marriages. Their relationships no longer lived up to their expectations. What started the revolution was not what is popularly called the women's movement, but the inability of men to be able to live up to the old culture image of the knight. This failure of men to be the knight in shining armor led to the revolution. The frustration felt by men is that they had no control over their own fate, although they were often blamed as if they were somehow responsible for everything that happened to them.

In addition, women began to realize city life, far from the old subsistence farms, offered them other marriage options. Sitting around and waiting for their first husbands to solve their financial problems was no longer an acceptable option. Women became assertive, not because they wanted to, but because they had no choice.

Not only were women disillusioned with the status quo and the failure of men to become knights, but also men found it increasingly impossible to deal with their diminished influence at home and inability to produce an income to provide for their families. As a result, both men and women felt the pressure of a world that was changing around them. At the same time, men and women found it was totally beyond their ability to control what had happened.

The first problem encountered with the increased divorce rate was the inability of the courts to handle the caseload. The old divorce laws limited the grounds of divorce to the three I's: incompetence, impotence, and infidelity. All at once, individuals began to realize that the old concept of "one, and only one" was a myth and there were other options for love. Rapidly, divorce lost its 1950's negative stigma. Since the majority of divorcees eventually wanted to remarry, no one was willing to step forward and admit impotence or incompetence, limiting the courts to concentrate on finding fault based on infidelity. As a result, distasteful and extensive proof trials put even consenting adults mutually desiring to end their marriages in awkward and difficult situations. As the case volume increased so too did the backlog. The solution to the bottleneck started in California with the introduction of no fault divorce. The concept quickly spread across the land as an integral part of the revolution.

In the meantime, daughters of World War II women dutifully followed the example of their mothers in blind faith and walked down the aisle to the altar. However, they quickly discovered the same reality as their mothers. This new generation of females wasted no time in joining the rush to the courthouse. They realized the plight of men had not changed in a generation and, unfortunately, they had married serfs of the village instead of knights with castles.

While no fault divorce initially alleviated the backlog in the divorce courts, it also encouraged others to file new divorce actions due to the elimination of fault. A wave of new cases soon flooded the country. In fact, there were times during the revolution when the numbers of divorces in this country exceeded the number of marriages. Too many people were entering the court system to maintain a negative stigma. Being divorced became the norm. Suddenly marital mistakes could be forgiven, and a new life could be found after a disastrous first marriage. Within a short period of time, our society went from a country where divorce was rare and taboo, to one where the failure to be divorced was rare and failed to carry the negative stigma. This dramatic change took place in little over a single generation, a rapid shift in social relations that was also revolutionary.

The net result of this new flood of divorces was a new class of urban poor made up of young divorced women with small children. This group remains one of the largest segments of society to this day and an important factor even after the revolution. The government was not totally oblivious to what was happening. Many laws were passed in the late 1960's through the 1970's in the form of consumer legislation intended to help the new urban poor. These new laws included the Truth in Lending Law, Fair Credit Reporting Act, The Real Estate Settlement Procedures Act, as well as a number of other distinctly pro-female employment related laws. The Equal Credit Opportunity Act (ECOA) was drafted expressly to help women face their new economic reality. So, much legislation comes down to pure economic necessity. Of all the legislation that helped women, ECOA was the most important law in the revolution because it dealt directly with the economics in their lives. Women needed to be able to borrow money to buy the necessities of life, and the vehicle of credit was essential to do so. Their very survival, just like that of men, now depended on access to credit. As is frequently the case, since women now had the right to vote, legislators had to act, just to stay in office. The power of the female vote acted as a catalyst for enacting favorable legislation for women.

As important as it was, the social revolution never reached the headlines because other events on the national and international stage dominated the available media time and space. However, the new social revolution was the more lasting of all the events faced by this country since the 1960's, while its impact went virtually unnoticed. The dilemma is that we still think in terms of the rigid stereotype of a male as head of the household. The male is still seen as dominant and in control over his family, consisting of his dutiful wife and children. We still see this old template as the model of American domestic life even though the world in which we now live has changed forever. Today, the myth of the two-parent family exists in less than 30% of American households.

The inconsistency between the reality of our daily lives and the old stereotyped images retained from before the revolution is so great that both men and women today feel stress, turmoil, and frustration. Until we realize a return to the old image of farm life is no longer possible and the role models inherited from them are no longer viable, men and women will continue to experience this stress, turmoil and frustration. The old subsistence farms have been plowed under to make way for an ever-growing expanse of new subdivisions. We keep looking back to the past for our ideal behavior models. Although the headlines of today like those of the past have a tendency to divert our attention from what is really going on around us, the struggle with the concept of the old lifestyle as an ideal is the major problem we face in our society today.

A broad, general exposure to the historical factors that led to the revolution against old social habits and customs should help one understand that the female drive for equality is based on simple economics. Poor employment prospects, not poor marriage prospects, are the most important issue for unmarried women, while full employment is now the greatest source of satisfaction for both men and women.

An understanding of the historical forces behind the rejection of our old culture should increase awareness of the ways that same old culture continues to restrict individuals personally today. Knowledge of the nature of the struggle against culture will increase each person's ability to survive in a world that has changed forever.

CHAPTER THREE: A NEW POINT OF VIEW

To illustrate how the revolution has changed our society forever, looking at the world from a new point of view helps cultivate a new understanding. The remainder of this book will use terms that are designed to change existing viewpoints not found in the same context anywhere else. These terms have been created solely to help describe the world in a way that will facilitate an understanding of how the two internal fable images affect our personal lives.

Becoming familiar with this new terminology and its meaning will help create a new perspective. With increased awareness of how old customs and traditions influence the behavior in both one's self and others, the new perspective will help to make better decisions on important issues. By observing the world from this new, fresh viewpoint, one may recognize areas where the danger of following old customs and practices automatically, without thought, can lead to unintended consequences.

Some terminology introduced in this book will be explained in context, but the following terms are not otherwise defined, so they are given special attention in this chapter. Based in the historical background, one may easily adopt them for use. As awareness of the danger of old customs increases so too will the ability to adjust to the application of these terms.

American Dark Ages:

That period of time from the founding of this country up to the year 1966. The selection of the end date for this period is tied to the participation of females in professional careers that never exceeded the 3 % level until the dramatic increase that began in 1966. The end of this period coincides with the beginning of the social revolution, as defined herein. The American Dark Ages was dominated by what is defined here as old culture thinking by both men and women. During this period, women saw themselves predominantly as housewives whose exclusive role in life was to raise a family and to be submissive to their husbands. Women were perceived by men as objects they possessed, as the bearer of children and subordinate housewives over whom men asserted dominion and control.

The majority of women who worked during this period did so only in entry-level temporary non-career positions to help support the family. Women also did not see themselves as individuals separate from their husbands. They saw themselves only in terms of the old images. During the American Dark Ages, neither men nor women had any real idea what it meant to be married. The perception of marriage was based on the behavior model of the old images and the conventional wedding album pictures that portrayed the marriage ceremony.

Social Revolution.

That period of time in this country beginning January 1, 1966 and ending on or about January 1, 2000, the date when female employment reached 50% of the total workforce. The changes brought about by the revolution continue today, but the dramatic rate of change that identified this period as a revolution has slowed. The key element of the revolution is the change in the way women perceive themselves. This change is evidenced by the dramatic increase in enrollment by females in professional degree programs in colleges and universities and the shift to long-term career objectives. Having a family changed from being the only or primary goal in life to becoming a part of daily life in addition to pursuit of personal goals.

Suddenly, a major percentage of the female population recognized themselves as separate, equal human beings with the same goals and objectives as men. Husbands were no longer thought of as objects, but as equals and partners in life. Marriage became less of a life objective and was seen as a personal relationship held together by common interests and goals. Marriage became a relationship to be undertaken when and only when a person found a totally compatible partner.

The beginning date of the social revolution coincides with the end of the American Dark Ages and ends with the beginning of the Transition. The social revolution should not be confused with the Transition, which is ongoing and will continue indefinitely into the future, while the revolution ended on or about January 1, 2000. Many people see the revolution as the recognition of the emergence of the American female as a separate human being.

Revolution.

An abbreviated version of the term social revolution.

Castle.

This term is taken from the fable image story of the knight in shining armor. The use of this term serves as a substitute for the primary family residence or home, whether it is a condominium unit or a single-family residence. While cooperative units known as 'coops' are places where people reside and fit some aspects of the term, they are not held in true ownership and the concepts addressed in the technical chapters on estates in land do not include these types of possessory arrangements.

Old Culture.

This term is used to refer to those persons who see themselves and their spouses in terms of the two images described in the last chapter. Specifically this term includes those individuals where, on marriage, women are merged with their husbands to the extent the husband is often seen as the survivor and the woman disappears as a separate person. Those persons who fit this classification see the husband as the breadwinner and provider in the relationship while the wife is both subordinate and submissive and usually limited to the role of housewife.

Both men and women are seen in the typical polarized stereotype roles illustrated by the fabled images. In these images the extremes of masculinity and femininity for the old culture people are the idealized behavior model for their lives. The term is somewhat misleading because there are millions of people in this country, both men and women, who fit the definition today. The term has no relevance to race, color, religion, national origin, sex, marital status, age, or income. The defining element is how that person perceives themselves and their spouse. The term refers only to those people who are locked into the stereotypical thinking and model their behavior in terms of the internalized images.

Knight in Shining Armor.

This term refers to males as envisioned in the old culture images. A knight is the sole breadwinner who is lord and master of his home and sees himself as protector of his family. All the characteristics that are associated with the images apply to this term.

Prince Millibucks Charming.

A symbolic personification of the knight in shining armor of the old culture images.

Prince.

An abbreviation of Prince Millibucks Charming, the knight in the images.

Pauper Princess.

A symbolic personification of the orphan girl represented in the old culture images. The term will be used to both describe how men of the old culture see women, as well as how women of the old culture see themselves. This term represents how most men and women perceived females in the American Dark Ages. The term pauper refers not just to her need to find a husband for economic support but to the fact her existence in the old culture is impoverished mentally, emotionally, and socially, restricted to the subordinate role of housewife.

Princess.

A shortened version of the pauper princess.

Transitional.

This term is used to describe those persons, both men and women, who are consciously rejecting the old culture while still continuing to show some outward characteristics of old culture habits and customs. Transitionals are constantly changing as they distance themselves from the old culture. They will continue to increase the degree to which they reject the old culture over time. Their move away from the old behavior stereotype is permanent as they struggle to find a new self-perception.

The key element that identifies them is that they see men and women as equal, capable human beings, just differing physically and biologically. Transitionals cannot be called new culture people because they still show characteristics of the old images and to some degree unconsciously retain the old images.

The Transition.

That period of time from January 1, 2000, the end of the social revolution, that will continue to the beginning of the new culture. There is no way to estimate how long this period will last, but it will end only when the new culture replaces any and all remnants of the old one, and will remain with us as long as the old culture remains a part of our internal self perception. The Transition is likely to continue for several more generations.

New Culture.

A time in the distant future when human life will be richer and more rewarding than the time in which we live. The way people act and think will be very different from today. No one living today could be described as a new culture person. Transitionals are in the process of shedding the old culture but they are not new culture people because they unconsciously continue to carry the old images still affecting their behavior. The new culture is still a long way off. A hypothetical description of the new culture is any one's best guess as to what the characteristics of what the new culture will bring. No one can predict what the new culture will be like. All we know is that the old culture images and habits will be gone forever.

The Premise.

The premise refers to the assumption that the images described here are in fact the core of our culture. The validity of the premise is completely unknown. The premise is simply a device created to help increase awareness of the dangers of old customs and traditions on our personal lives.

Jousting:

The knight's equivalent of going to work.

Social Orientation:

The condition of being either old culture or transitional.

Making poor Adam whole again:

This phrase refers to the internal need of both old culture males and females to be married, and the need to encourage others to do the same. The reference is used with males when they are looking for an old culture wife who fits the image of the pauper princess. The reference is used with females when they are looking for a husband who fits the image of the knight in shining armor. The phrase is used to emphasize that the search for an old culture spouse is for an object as a means to reach the goal of living in accordance with the old culture images. Individual personalities and differences have no meaning in the search for the stereotype behavior pattern.

The remainder of this book incorporates the above terms exclusively as aids to help increase awareness of the dangers of a reliance on old habits and customs. Once exposed to these terms in context, the reader should find an increased awareness of old culture habits and behaviors and gain a new understanding for the future. However, while reading this book, use this chapter as a guide to refresh an understanding of the terms and how they are used. Reread this chapter at any time before proceeding to the next concept or chapter.

CHAPTER FOUR: THE GREAT DIVIDE

    The definitions in the last chapter of both old culture and transitional people provide only a brief introduction to the most important aspect of the revolution. In the American Dark Ages, people in this country were basically all alike with respect to social orientation. During that time, this was a homogenous nation made up of old culture individuals. There were a few transitional people, but they were rare. More importantly, they had no impact on the social consciousness of the nation. The revolution altered society forever. One of the primary changes appeared in the rapid growth in the number of transitional people. The development of these two different types of social orientation created what is referred to here as the "Great Divide."
    Our population can now be clearly characterized by this split into two groups of social orientation, one consisting of transitional people and the other, old culture people. These two groups are totally incompatible and opposite in the way they perceive and react to the world around them. The most important issue on the journey to increased awareness includes understanding the significant differences between these two social orientations and developing the skill to detect the defining characteristics that identify them. The ability to classify people by social orientation is important because the only strategy to deal with members of the opposite classification is avoidance. They have nothing in common with each other. The quality of life on a day-to-day basis will depend on one's ability to differentiate between the old culture and transitional social orientation to avoid the continuous clashes faced by those less observant.
    First, determine the category a person belongs in and then the observer will find certain aspects of human behavior are predictable within each

classification. However, since both groups exist across our country, be aware that social orientation is not determined simply by geographic location or physical appearance. In fact, none of the common classifications such as race, national origin, age, gender, or other observable characteristics are of any help whatsoever. Unfortunately, the only successful way to deal with the great divide is to watch how people behave and listen to what they say.

On the other hand, apply these terms with great care. Sometimes it is difficult to accurately classify an individual based only on an initial meeting. For example, there may be degrees to which a person is transitional or old culture. In fact, many people are transitional rather than new culture simply because they continue to retain a few of the old culture characteristics. In the process of attempting to classify people, one may add up the number of old culture charactcristics attributable to a person, then add up the number of transitional characteristics and compare the totals as a way of assigning the person to one category or the other. Remember, we are in transition and some individuals will not be clearly one social orientation or the other, but various blends of both. As a result, unfortunately, determining social orientation is not so easy. There is more involved than just scoring numbers of characteristics. However, the core element of what distinguishes these two social styles is the way they think. How people think about others is the key to each category.

Generally speaking, old culture people see marriage as the merger together of the male and female as one, and they usually see the female as merged back into the male. The net effect is that women are seen as truly subordinate to men. On the other hand, transitional people see males and females as totally separate human beings with different biological systems. The obvious biological differences between the sexes are recognized, but transitionals see these differences as inconsequential compared to the degree to which males and females are alike socially. Old culture people see biological differences as justification for male superiority.

Transitionals will counter all the studies that emphasize biological differences between the sexes with the fact that of all the possible human emotions not one applies exclusively to one gender. They conclude that, in spite of genetic differences, men and women are more alike than they are different. Thus, both sexes should be treated equally in all respects. In fact, transitionals will point out that what distinguishes us as a species from all others that have ever lived on this earth is that human beings are goal seeking. *Homo sapiens* must have dreams, aspirations, and objectives for our lives to have meaning. Transitionals will further say that we are happiest, and most satisfied when we are busy striving towards some vision outside of ourselves. What is important on the journey to heightened awareness is that this special goal-seeking characteristic is equally prevalent for both males and females.

Old Culture people do not have personal goals. Instead, they willingly sacrifice personal objectives to model their lives in terms of the rigid behavior dictated by the old culture images. The old culture female sees her only purpose in life idealized by the pauper princess in the image. At best, she wants only to be a good housewife and mother. Transitional women see the world as full of opportunities and reject the stereotype behavior patterns of the old culture.

To further demonstrate the depth of the division between these two social orientations, the lists below are included to summarize some of the more common characteristics attributable to each group:

Old Culture Characteristics

Old culture people are not health conscious. In the fabled image, everyone lives forever, happily ever after. Modeling their day-to-day lives in terms of the image of the knight and princess is their sole and only objective. As a result, the following are common characteristics of old culture people:

> Excessive smoking
> Excessive drinking
> Non-genetic obesity
> Lack of exercise

Old culture people are often heavily involved in non-participatory sports and maintain strong identity and loyalty to specific teams and players. They achieve emotional gratification from the success of others through observation. There is no tie between the success of sports professionals and the personal lives of old culture people. Yet, spectator sports play an integral part of their daily existence.

Old culture people watch television and listen to the radio so they can absorb the thoughts and ideas of others, because they have none of their own.

Old culture people believe children should be seen but not heard.

Old culture people are joiners and followers and are found participating in social groups. They enjoy being in large crowds of people like themselves.

Group identification and a sense of belonging are very important to their personal identity.

Old culture people see no reason to improve themselves. If the world would only go back to the way things were several decades ago, back in the American Dark Ages, everything would be perfect. The world needs to change, not them.

Old culture people have only one objective in life, maintaining a lifestyle modeled after the old culture images.

Old culture people do not accept responsibility for anything. Everything that goes wrong is always someone else's fault.

Old culture people have a thinly disguised sense of insecurity. They need emotional support of others like themselves.

Old culture people are oblivious to their social orientation. They are unaware that others are different from themselves in the way they perceive the world around them.

Old culture people believe women are genetically inferior to men and think women should be restricted to subordinate and submissive activities.

Old culture people believe children are possessions of their parents.

Old culture people are quick to alter facts and ignore laws that do not fit their own needs and viewpoint. Modeling their lives in the stereotype behavior pattern overrides everything else.

Old culture people focus on petty details and cannot see the big picture.

Transitional characteristics

Transitional people are conscious about their health. To accomplish their goals and dreams, they recognize the need to maintain their bodies because their body is the only vehicle through which they can succeed.

Transitionals are participants in active sports activities. They may occasionally observe sports events involving professionals, but they prefer active participation rather than passive. They have no identification with professional teams or players.

Transitionals avoid television and radio shows where they are forced to absorb the thoughts and opinions of others. They concentrate on developing their own ideas.

Transitionals are interested in promoting constructive change, not just for themselves, but also for everyone else.

Transitional people believe children should be encouraged to express themselves as young as possible.

Transitionals avoid crowds. They feel more comfortable by themselves. They often feel they do not belong in any specific group.

Transitionals are obsessive about self-improvement and bettering themselves to deal with the changing world around them.

Transitionals are goal seeking. Their entire existence consists of setting goals and seeking ways to accomplish them. They do not accept existing or traditional barriers to goal accomplishment. They often find creative ways to achieve their goals, overcoming obstacles.

Transitionals accept responsibility even when something is not their own fault. They know they grow by taking responsibility, and they learn from past errors.

Transitionals obtain their emotional needs from within themselves and are independent of the opinions of others.

Transitionals are very aware that all people are unique individuals and they are also aware that they are very different from old culture people.

Transitionals see men and women as equal members of the human race, notwithstanding biological differences.

Transitionals see children as unique human beings from the day they are born. They see parents' roles as custodians with the responsibility of overseeing the growth of children until they are adults on their own.

Transitionals build their future from a foundation based on existing facts and laws.

Transitionals are always focused on the big picture and do not let details and petty issues divert them from their goals.

These comparisons are but a few of many that could be listed. The objective here is not to create an exhaustive description of the two orientations, but to draw attention to the depth of the gulf that exists between them. Obviously, pairing the two groups up for light conversation at a cocktail party would not be a success, but it should also be clear that opposing social styles would not make good marriage partners.

Transitionals are predictable in that they consciously avoid the old images even though they may not yet be consciously aware of their classification or its specific characteristics. People may qualify as transitional even though they still unconsciously carry the old images making it difficult to identify them from observable characteristics unconsciously retained from the old culture images. However, once the process of rejecting the old images starts, it does not stop. Transitionals will continue to change throughout their lives. An old culture characteristic seen in a transitional person one year may be missing altogether a year later.

Transitionals are on a journey leading to the new culture even though they do not know exactly where the journey will lead. Realistically they will vary individually in the degree to which they reject the old culture. However, trying to subdivide transitionals by degree is not useful due to the characteristic of continual change. Thus, any attempt at sub-classification is futile. Sub-classification serves no purpose in increasing awareness of the dangers of the influence of culture.

On the other hand, an old culture person is likely to think, act, and speak exactly the same way over time. Subdividing old culture people into two basic categories is possible. Simply stated, one group consists of those who believe that females merge into males through marriage and women no longer exist separate and apart from their husbands. The other group consists of those who do not believe in the total disappearance of the female, but do believe that men and women are merged together as one on marriage. These old culture distinctions will be relevant in certain aspects of property ownership, and will be addressed at that time. In all other respects, any reference to the old culture orientation will include both groups.

Old culture people are not true individuals. They find their identity through others and think only in terms of living their lives using the images as a guide. In fact, living in conformity with the images is their only objective in life. This focus creates a void when they have free time. They fill their free time with passive activities where there are no personal objectives to gain. To many old culture people, work is simply a necessary evil and consists mostly of dull, boring routine.

Since old culture people simply model their lives as close to the images as possible, they have no other interests to fill their lives. Thus, they need passive activities that take their minds off the routine of work. If they have a stated objective, it is retirement, another activity without goals. Old culture people also have an obsession with money as an end in and of itself instead of a means to achieve a goal. Old culture people have no other way to evaluate their successes or failures in life, but to measure their success in terms of money.

Transitionals are active rather than passive people. They go to great effort to build a career that coincides with their interests and do not think in terms of "work." They earn their income from activities that they enjoy. They receive their greatest satisfaction from what they do for a living. Money plays a secondary role in the life of a transitional person where money is used to help achieve their goals. Their primary satisfaction is in doing things that have value to society and to them personally. The following statement by a transitional woman after spending a few days with an old culture family may help further illustrate the great divide:

> *My experience was enlightening but somewhat frightening. All the houses in the suburbs look the same to me. I found it difficult to tell one house from another. The people in suburbia dress, act, and think alike. They share the same interests in watching and discussing events in which they do not participate and have no impact on their personal lives.*
>
> *Their lives are routine. They go to and from work each day in a set pattern. Evenings and Sundays are allocated to watching sports on television if they do not have tickets to attend the actual event. They live their lives through their children who maintain dreams and aspirations until they become of age when they give up their goals in favor of adopting the same lifestyle of their parents.*

Of course this woman is assuming all children will be old culture and willingly spend their lives living out the same old culture images as their parents. The world has changed, and it is far more likely that the children mentioned will be transitional and seek independent lives free from the narrow thinking of their parents.

Transitional people are more likely to listen to classical music that helps inspire their own thoughts, and they watch television programs that challenge their minds rather than programs where the viewers absorb the conclusions of others. Transitionals are aware of what they are doing and why they are doing it, whereas old culture people react without thought, unaware of the implications of what they are doing or why.

The comparison lists should help illustrate the differences between these two social orientations to aid in developing the ability to identify and avoid the dangers created by the old culture in your personal life. In the struggle with culture, everyone is on their own. No one can change other people, and no one can do for others what they cannot do for themselves. Everyone feels anxiety, stress and conflict, but every resolution of the social struggle is a personal one.

The transitional experiences stronger emotional turmoil than the old culture person. The more transitional characteristics one has, the greater the gap between the new life and the old culture images used to evaluate appropriate behavior. Old culture images increase the stress and frustration individuals feel due to the fact the real world is moving further away from the old images and old behavior patterns are no longer appropriate. This results in conflict with the transitional and the old culture surrounding them in their daily lives.

Once aware of the dangers of the images, one is able to work towards the only solution possible, a conscious reduction of the power of the images over thought and behavior. Survival in the world today requires developing the ability to resist the influence of culture. The only way to do so is to be aware of its power.

In the American Dark Ages, the old culture social orientation was dominant in our country. The revolution gave birth to the transitional person as a major force in modern American life. Although there are many more transitional people today than there were before the revolution, the images of the old culture are still buried deeply within every living person in our country today. A middle-aged woman made the following comment:

> *I just got married for the second time. I want you to know I'm very transitional. This time I kept my name.*

After being asked what name she would give her child, she responded:

> *You have to give the child the name of the father. You must support the family.*

Her response was expected. This is the Transition, not the new culture, and transitional females usually make the same decision. What was momentarily surprising was that she responded to the question automatically without thinking. She was not as transitional as she would like others to believe. The response to the question by a transitional person would be to first pause, then respond something like the following:

> *That's a good question. I never thought about it before.*

Ultimately, the transitional woman will most likely make the same decision as the woman who made the comment, but the response to the question is never automatic or instantaneous. About every six months, since the beginning of the revolution, a new self-help book written by a woman for other women reaches the bookstore shelves. The theme of "how to find a husband" is always the same but differs only as variation of the same theme. These books are old culture in orientation and written by old culture females for an old culture audience. What often appears surprising is their appeal to women who have professional careers. If we are in the Transition, why are these books so popular?

The answer is the same as in the case of the woman who had not changed her name. There are many women who think they are transitional or who appear to be, when in fact they are not. Just because a woman has good job or retains her maiden name on marriage does not make her transitional in social orientation. The key to whether an individual has crossed the great divide is in the way the person thinks, not the specific characteristics that are attributable to one orientation or the other. Sometimes women say:

> *I pretend to enjoy sex with him when I have to. I am willing to make any sacrifice to have a family.*

This is an old culture concept, where women see men as a means to an end, not as unique individuals. This comment goes to the core of old culture thinking. Old culture thinking exists in both men and women. It is true that the old culture male is very preoccupied with a woman's physical appearance, but the woman who thinks that sex and physical attraction is what marriage is all about misses the most important element of the old culture concept. In the old culture marriage, sex is the only thing that is shared. Both partners use each other as a means to live the old culture lifestyle. The real issue is the need of the old culture male to assert mental dominion and control over his spouse. Physical domination is just one aspect of this need to control. Unless women understand this simple fact, they will not appreciate the concept of the merger of the female back into the male, and they will miss the true significance of the disappearance of the female as a separate individual through the marriage ceremony.

When the old culture male says he is "looking for a wife," he is looking for an object, not a person. He is looking for a stereotype female who will live her life automatically behaving in accordance with his internal cultural images. In short, he does not want her to think as an individual. In essence, the old culture wife is a necessary means to an end for a lifestyle in the image of the knight. The male's need for total dominance over the female's mental independence is the core of old culture male thinking. The professional career woman who says she has decided to start looking for a husband is either old culture or she does not understand the great divide. Clearly, she does not have a clear picture of who she is. If this is the case, the future of divorce attorneys remains assured.

Transitional people are not cold, unemotional misfits. Most would like to have families, but only if they meet the right partner. On their journey through life, having a family is something a transitional person does if the circumstances are right. Having a family and a home life are not their end objective. To sacrifice your life to have a family is strictly old culture thinking. Either the individual finds the right relationship or does not. In either case, the transitional person continues to pursue their individual goals and aspirations.

The difference in the way old culture and transitional individuals think is not a line drawn in the sand, but a deep, wide chasm. The mental bridge required to cross the great divide works only one way. Once safely across, one can never go backwards. However, once across the divide, one may experience a profound awakening and freedom from the rigid role models of the past. Because those with an old culture orientation are frequently in opposition to those in transition, excessive contact across the great divide often leads to adverse personal and financial consequences to the transitional person. In extreme cases, the interrelationship between people with opposite social orientations may even lead to physical violence. For this reason, identification of old culture characteristics in others as quickly and expediently as possible is important to develop techniques to deal with them or avoid them.

Becoming more aware of these contrasting views of the world allows one to detect one or the other of these orientations in every television show, movie, newspaper, book and person they meet. Thankfully, once one is aware of the visible and audible characteristics of social orientation, the ability to determine social orientation becomes less difficult. Developing the skill to reach a firm conclusion is important because the orientation of others will dictate the type of relationship one may be capable of having with them.

Sometimes by listening to others when they speak, one may be able to identify social orientation from their conversation. For example, the following comment was overheard at a shopping mall:

> *I don't know, Mildred. If I were you, I wouldn't do anything. I wouldn't rock the boat. Don't forget he's the man of the house. Personally, I'd just do whatever he says.*

The speaker clearly revealed her social orientation as strictly old culture. She believes totally in the concept that marriage merges the female back into the male with the male as the sole survivor. What more is there about Mildred that we don't know? If she were transitional, she would be making a major error. Transitionals do not ask old culture people questions about how to handle interpersonal relations. They know the answer will only be an old culture response like the one in our example. However, far more likely, Mildred is old culture too, because transitional women do not ask their spouses for permission to do anything. They simply keep their spouses informed of what they are doing. For example:

> *Ted, I'm going to the mall with Sally. We may see a movie so I'll be late. You're on your own for dinner. There's plenty to eat in the refrigerator. Help yourself.*

Social orientation is not determined by age, gender or any other physical characteristic. Old culture thinking can appear in young people, just as easily as in older people born back in the American Dark Ages. The following comment made by a young woman is strictly old culture thinking:

> *We've been married for almost two years, and he always has some wild, new idea. I wish he'd settle down. He has a good job. He should realize his career is our future.*

Learning to identify social orientation by watching television in the privacy of the home is good practice. However, watching television provides the opportunity to see one or more of a number of similar television shows that will stand out because of the subject matter. These shows often consist of three parts where young female contestants are competing for the attention of a handsome young man who has inherited untold millions. In these shows, Prince Millibucks Charming has been lifted right out of the story of the knight in shining armor. As the central character, he always appears in search of a wife. In the first segment, he reduces the number of pauper princesses by eliminating those who obviously do not fit the role of princess in his image. In the second segment, his role becomes more difficult. The clues that show any hint of individual personalities are more difficult to use to eliminate unwanted pauper princesses to be. Over the course of the show, Prince Millibucks manages to eliminate all but two candidates, carefully screening for all the old culture characteristics. In the final segment, the prince selects his "one and only" followed by a fancy storybook wedding at a five star resort on an exotic tropical island, all pure fantasy, right out of the story books.

Clearly these shows are scripted out of the American Dark Ages, careful renditions of the old culture images. For some reason, these shows are extremely popular with the under thirty crowd. This causes us to wonder if the revolution of the last three decades has simply evaporated.

In each show, the prince is always young, handsome, but clearly, old culture in social orientation. He handles himself very carefully trying not to give himself away, but he is looking for a pauper princess to whisk off to his castle in a limousine. This scenario is classic old culture.

When watching such shows closely, we wonder what the true motivation is for each of the pauper princesses. Could they be participating just for the fancy wardrobe, meals, exotic trips, financial remuneration provided by the sponsors, or are they actresses on a movie shoot? We find it difficult to believe they are actually participating because they are looking for an old culture husband, right out of the images of the American Dark Ages. For these young people, what happened to the education and professional careers of the competing princesses? Can their motivation be as empty as desiring just to win the prince?

The real story should follow the lives of the princesses who were left back on the steps of the village inn, the ones not chosen. Would they go back to the real world of college and professional jobs or would they simply go to the nearest singles bar and continue husband hunting in another direction? This is the Transition. The conclusion for the unsuccessful princesses might be that after this brief fling at playing pauper princess, they go back to work. Their participation in the show was just a fantastic dream, playing to the old fading images like a nostalgic old movie.

Of course, we may never know the true motivation of the pauper princesses, because the producers of these shows are not interested in that story. The old culture goal is locked into and clearly focused on the elaborate symbols of the wedding ceremony in the last segment. Development of a real interpersonal relationship between the lucky princess and the knight is limited to the short span of the program, hardly enough time to learn much more than each other's names. The only goal of the producers is the need to make poor Adam whole again through a lavish celebration of merger.

The conversations between the participants on these shows are always focused on the rings, the gown, the reception, and the limousine, all for a wedding to a person the lucky princess has known only from a few brief encounters in front of the cameras. At least, the lucky couple will not need a wedding album. They will have an entire television show to document the event.

Becoming more aware of the great divide may cause one to question the future of the winning princess after she is ushered through a storybook wedding right out of the old fables. How will she feel a year later, if the marriage lasts that long? What will her life be like married to Prince Charming? The prince's every move is easily predicted. He is on his best behavior, but his old culture orientation is thinly disguised. Will the lucky princess be as old culture as all the contestants are portrayed? More importantly, what will happen to her if she is old culture on her wedding day, but becomes transitional sometime after the ceremony, like so many other women in this country? If she does become aware of the different social orientations and begins to see herself as transitional, we can predict his reaction. She is likely to need a good lawyer and maybe even a restraining order. The important point here is that these shows set up a classic old culture pitfall that will be covered under the topic of individual ownership of property. Of course, these shows also illustrate how the focus of attention in every wedding is solely on the ceremony itself and not on the underlying personal issues involved in building a successful relationship designed to last a lifetime.

In fact, these types of shows don't cover any of the issues raised in this book. The single focus of attention is limited to finding a pauper princess for poor Adam so he can be made whole again in a traditional ceremony of merger. All that matters are the elaborate symbols, including the exotic location, the reception, the gown, the rings, and the limousine. The actors are selected as precise stereotypes out of the old culture images. Personal characteristics and individual circumstances have no relevance or value in the old culture. To ask about the real issues of what marriage means to the individuals involved is taboo. To ask real questions back in the American Dark Ages was to threaten the marriage ceremony and the very fabric of our culture.

Everyone would like to think we are safe in assuming these shows are interesting because they are mere fantasy. The castle is a distant image in the misty recesses of the minds of those in the audience. Keep an open mind to see how many of those who claim they are transitional actually still have a long ways to go. We are over thirty years into the Transition. Certainly, the vast majority of young women today are not living their lives in search of the old images. However, these shows are excellent examples of the modern application of the old culture. They make useful illustrations to study on the way to increased awareness of the power of the old culture on personal behavior.

Becoming aware of how old customs and habits influence life today, we might conclude that parents of the children born back in the American Dark Ages never told their children some critical things. That is where the problems began. When those children were very young, their parents told them about myths, and magic, i.e. fairy tales. Parents told their children about Santa Claus, the Tooth Fairy, the Easter Bunny, and all the rest. These trusting children believed the stories were real, in the innocence of their youth. Those children may even remember, not so many years later, when their parents looked at them in a new light and told them they were growing up. Parents at that time were very concerned what would happen to their children if they still believed in Santa Clause at age eighteen. Those parents told their children they had to face reality so they could live balanced lives as adults. All the old myths were destroyed, all except one, the story about knights in shining armor and pauper princesses.

Those children grew up with that myth intact, even when they were eighteen and went off to work or college and started careers. Males learned a trade so they could become knights. Females became husband hunters so they could move into suburban castles that replaced the old subsistence farms. In the American Dark Ages, no right-minded father encouraged his daughter to get a real education in a professional career. That simply was not done. Besides, a career and profession would put her femininity in doubt. Her father knew she would never find a husband exhibiting such behavior or having such goals.

The children of the American Dark Ages saw it all. They got married, divorced, remarried, on and on, stumbling after the images preserved all those years, looking for princesses and knights doing their best to ignore the reality surrounding them. In fact, they're still trying to hold their lives together today, wondering what happened and where they went wrong. They are oblivious to the fact the world just isn't the same place it was years ago. The world has changed, but they haven't changed with it.

Their parents never told them the old culture stories were a myth because they couldn't. They were old culture, and the myth was all they ever knew. The old images were what they had been told as part of their culture, and these images had been passed down from generation to generation without thinking, right up to the social revolution. Those children, now middle-aged adults, are wiser now, or at least they'd like to think they are. They'd like to think they've learned the lesson that the story of knights and pauper princesses was, in the end, just another childhood fable. However, today, most of these children are too old to learn. The following comment describing their plight was overheard at a golf course:

> *Did you hear about Bill? His daughter is getting married. He promised her a big, fancy wedding here at the club. He figures it's going to set him back about 20 grand. She's been living with the guy for two years, but Bill hasn't even met him yet.*

Why do brides wear white wedding gowns in today's world? The answer certainly can't be tied to biological purity. That went out with the social revolution and the end of the American Dark Ages. Still, young women go to the altar in white. Could it be the white wedding gown goes back to the old culture story when the knight first sweeps the princess up onto his horse? Could it be that he is saving her? What if the white wedding gown is more a symbol of saving her from a life of poverty with the future that women may dread the most, ending up on the street barefoot and in rags. Could that white gown be more a symbol of cleanliness? Is the knight saving her from a life of dirt and grime, and she is being swept up to the clean castle far above the village? Does the gown symbolize that she will never again fear ending up dirty on the streets?

It's easy to understand why women in the American Dark Ages made the compromises they did. Back then, there were few alternatives to getting married. In those days women didn't want to hear any questions that would even remotely threaten the ceremony. When he "popped the question," she often accepted without a clue of what marriage meant beyond the champagne, the rings, the album, the guest list, the reception and all the rest of the trappings. Poor Adam was no different. He was asking the question without a clue that he needed to make poor Adam whole again. On the other hand, she only saw the ceremony, while his attention was fixed, at least unconsciously, on the old culture picture of the knight in shining armor. If he didn't have a princess he couldn't be a knight.

There were a few exceptions where wealthy parents slid prenuptial agreements into their son's hands to protect the fancy car, the yacht, the airplane, and the apartment building or stock portfolio left by grandfather. Other than that, no one had a clue what marriage meant. In those days, the American Dark Ages truly lived up to the name. Any discussion of the details involved in marriage was basically taboo.

Most young men and women learn about sex from their peer group, not their parents or teachers. In addition, they learned by experimentation in the backseat of a car in the local drive-in theater. Any discussion about sexually transmitted diseases was done after the fact in the doctor's office when it was too late to talk about prevention. Times have changed. Those old drive in theaters have disappeared along with the American Dark Ages of which they were so much a part. In fact, back then entire lives could be characterized as groping in the dark. One woman's comment makes a good example of what was going on back then:

> *When I was young, the thing to do was to go out on blind dates. Looking back I can see how blind we really were. I wonder how many marriages, like mine, were based on the blind leading the*

> blind? I told my daughter, the key to developing a successful marriage does not come from hit or miss dating, but from knowing who you are and spending your time with someone like yourself. Maybe she can learn from my mistakes.

The really sad part of the American Dark Ages was that the old culture image of the castle came true for many married women. They found out too late that their husbands were out advancing their careers, and the kids were in school learning all about the wonders of the world beyond the home. In the meantime, the princess was alone, trapped in the suburban castle. Even more restraining for the princesses of the American Dark Ages, most families had only one car. The pauper princess was truly isolated in the castle with no present, no future, no dreams or goals, just the monotony of doing the same household duties over and over, forever after, doing the laundry, making dinners, washing dirty dishes, cleaning the castle... Once the kids went to school, life at home was as empty and as isolated as the vision the castle on the hill represented.

On the other hand, the knight spent his life working late, proudly skipping vacations believing he was dedicating his life to providing for his princess. He was convinced his princess was content to be protected in the castle, waiting for him to come home. All too often he drove himself to an early death believing up to the end he had done the right thing. Unfortunately, he left his princess truly alone in the castle, too old to seek another knight, and certainly too old to seek a future for herself. In reality, they were both trapped by the images of the old culture myth. During all those years, the wedding dress, worn only once, remained packed away in mothballs. The wedding album, collecting dust on a shelf in the living room, was untouched since first examined after the wedding many years ago.

Some people say the housewives of the American Dark Ages took menial jobs to help make ends meet. Some say a job, no matter how low paying, gave the princess freedom from the silent economic control of their husbands. All the reasons given have some degree of validity, but the job also helped the family buy a second car so the princess could escape from the castle and drive back down to the village to meet her friends once or twice a week. As a result, she then had someone to talk to.

Human beings are social beings. We all need contact with other people. Life alone in the castle for the princess was artificial. Freedom from isolation was just as important as the money in her motivation to work. Putting a wall phone in the kitchen with a long cord just wasn't enough to solve the need for interpersonal contact. The princess of the

American Dark Ages didn't find out until after marriage that knights didn't talk about what he did during his workday. When he came home from work, he mumbled through dinner then sat in his stuffed lounge chair by the hearth. He would either read the newspaper or watch sports on television. Both activities left the princess just as alone as she was when the knight went to work in the morning. During preparations for the wedding, no one ever told the princess that a cardinal rule of knighthood is that knights never talk to princesses.

We will never know the extent that alcoholism played in the lives of the princesses of the American Dark Ages. The isolation and a life without goals or dreams left many princesses with no other way to cope. Many solved the problem by watching soap operas, reinforcing more stories of knights and princesses and mirroring the empty world of the lonely princess home alone in the castle. One woman's comment summarizes this chapter:

> *I remember the day I had crossed the great divide. I found myself staring at my wedding ring. For the first time, I saw it as a reminder that I was not free, and I was the possession of someone else. I felt belittled, diminished, even repressed.*
>
> *I'm still married, but I no longer wear my ring. Somehow, not wearing that ring gives me a sense of freedom I didn't know before.*

Being aware of the significance of the differences between transitional and old culture thinking, one can identify these attitudes by listening to what people say and watching what they do. Learning how to make this determination will aid in detecting the social orientation in every show, book, paper, or other media as well as in every person we meet. Becoming aware that cultural orientation can act as a prison and create a false security is a startling revelation for the enlightened individual. Then the enlightened individual can make an informed decision to accept or reject old culture thinking that the subconscious images represent. The Transition will continue on its journey to the new culture in spite of the individual. To prosper and survive, the individual needs to knowingly develop the skills to deal with the customs and habits of either social orientation. Whether the individual develops this awareness, the changes in our social environment will continue. Developing awareness of these social orientations and the variations between them will aid in making appropriate decisions for the life style the individual chooses. Successfully dealing with other people and property ownership issues will be easier to handle with solid knowledge backing up the decision. The impact of awareness of cultural issues runs deep in the social fabric of our culture. Every decision individuals make will have a long lasting impact in the life of that individual. Making an informed, rational decision, knowing the consequences and implications of that decision, rather than automatic responses based on deep seated cultural customs, will help the individual make better decisions based on the needs and circumstances of the persons involved.

CHAPTER FIVE: CREDIT CLASH WITH CULTURE

During the American Dark Ages, women did not understand the importance of credit until the social revolution. This is not surprising since they did not earn or handle the money. However, as soon as they became aware of the need for credit, they found that no law created a specific right to receive it. In this country, credit is a privilege for which individuals must qualify, and must be earned. Webster's II New Riverside University Dictionary defines financial credit as:

> Reputation for solvency and integrity entitling a party to be trusted in buying or borrowing.
>
> Confidence in a buyer's ability and intention to fulfill financial obligations.
>
> Time allowed for payment for something sold on trust.
>
> An amount placed by a bank at the disposal of a client

Credit is a term derived from the Latin word "credo" which very loosely means, "to believe in." In essence, this is what credit is all about. Credit is the ability to obtain goods and services immediately in exchange for a promise to pay the agreed price at some time in the future. Sometimes the seller of the goods or services directly extends credit to the buyer. In other cases, a third party credit provider pays the seller. Then the borrower's repayment obligation is owed to the third party.

To understand how credit is made available, the borrower needs to know that the amount of credit available is a function of his/her credit rating. The credit rating is determined by a credit report. In our society, a credit report is a written document providing information on both the willingness and ability of the applicant to repay debt. Credit reports are neither magic nor are they made up of strange unfathomable secrets. They are in fact quite straightforward and include such things as:

>Background information on prior loans.
>Terms and balances of exiting loans.
>Analysis of payment performance on all present and past loans
>Adverse credit history of any kind.
>Recent credit inquiries by other lenders.
>Local public information including such things as:
>>Judgments
>>Liens
>>Lawsuits
>>Criminal records

These credit reports include an overall rating or what is referred to as opinion of credit or risk of non-payment. This rating is the estimated potential that the applicant might not be able or desire to repay debt. Credit reports provide sufficient information for lenders to make credit decisions.

Credit ratings are often reflected in the form of a credit scoring system. The credit scoring system is a statistical system used by lenders to rate applicants using the various factors anticipating repayment based on past credit history. Credit ratings consist of the evaluation of creditworthiness based on the above factors. Essentially, a credit rating is a creditor's expression of trust or confidence in the borrower.

Basic credit issues include the integrity of the borrower, or the history of paying an obligation as agreed, and the capacity or ability to repay a future debt no matter what the desire. Because unanticipated events can change the borrower's ability or willingness to repay debt, the creditor is always taking a risk, so part of the analysis of credit for the lender involves the cost of undertaking this unknown risk.

The best way to monitor and nurture one's credit rating is to periodically check the status and accuracy of the credit report. There are services that will help the borrower obtain a copy of a current credit report. Credit bureaus maintain credit information and provide this information to lenders for a fee. A rule of thumb for credit is to obtain and check the accuracy of this report once a year. If credit is used frequently, check the credit data more frequently.

The image of marriage as the merger of the male and female together as one is part of our culture. However, it is important to know that our society has never assigned a credit rating or identity to people who are married as one. The rating of each person as an individual is handled separately. Our society looks at combined credit capacity only when both spouses apply for credit together as joint applicants, where one spouse acts as a guarantor or cosigner for the other. Even in those cases where both spouses are involved, creditors simply look at the aggregate capacity of both individuals added together. All ratings and records are kept only in the name of individual persons, under the individual's social security number.

Credit is used for several reasons: necessity, convenience, and credit development, or maintenance. People in the third world look at this country as rich, but we know better. If Americans had to pay cash for automobiles, houses, and expensive capital goods, we would not be able to own these items until we were ready for retirement. What makes these large capital purchases accessible to most of us when we are young is credit. This is equally true for both males and females.

We use credit through access devices such as credit cards and special and regular checking accounts. These and other devices provide a convenient way to allow us to carry less cash with us on a day-to-day basis. Having to carry several thousand dollars at all times would be awkward, dangerous, and inconvenient. In addition, the time when credit is really needed usually occurs when there is not enough cash on hand. A credit card or other device that allows access to a credit line is much more convenient than cash.

Because both the necessity and convenience of credit are so important to our way of life, we often think of credit ratings and credit lines as assets, almost to the same extent as having cash on hand. A credit rating and credit lines aren't what we normally think of as an asset, but they are often just as important. Knowing that one has a good credit rating and a limit as high as possible available is a necessity in our economic environment. Never knowing when an emergency may arise where credit helps solve the emergency, is not just convenient, it has become a necessity. Frequently, some married woman may say:

> *Why should I do anything? I'm a housewife. My husband takes care of everything. I don't need credit. For me, a credit rating is meaningless.*

First, there are untold hundreds of thousands of incidents in this country each year that have a significant economic impact on both the primary individual as well as those closely related to them. Since such events are not limited to any specific age, gender or other group, these emergencies often create an immediate need for credit. To be prepared for sudden emergencies is a necessity. One of the best ways to prepare for the unexpected is by having a good credit line available. The following comment demonstrates one woman's approach to credit:

> *I apply for credit in my own name everywhere I can and for as much as I can get. Many times I don't need credit now, but I'm sure one of these days I will. I don't use cash unless I absolutely have to. I use credit whenever I can to maintain the credit lines that I have obtained. I pay my debts within the first billing cycle so I minimize any costs to maintain my credit. It gives me peace of mind to know credit is available.*
>
> *In an emergency, credit is like having money in the bank. Not having access to money when I need it is my real concern.*

To be prepared for those emergencies when available credit becomes important, some simple ways to handle economic affairs whether independent or totally dependent on a spouse's income or single and independent follow:

1. Decide on one specific name you want to use for all purposes.
2. Once you have selected the standard name be sure all personal identification shows the same name. Documents to review include:
   A. Drivers license.
   B. Passport
   C. Social Security Card
   D. Credit cards
   E. Voter's registration
   F. Membership cards
3. Open a checking account in your name only, using this same standard name, and use the account from time to time. The balance on hand is not as important as having the account open and ready to use.

4. Open a savings account in your name only using this same standard name.
5. Open at least one credit account with a bank that is accepted at most locations throughout the country. Apply for the maximum credit line the creditor will approve.
6. Open at least one specific convenient department store account with the maximum credit line the retailer will allow.
7. At least annually, order a copy of your credit report from a credit-reporting agency and check it for inaccuracies or fraudulent activity
8. Check the address on all accounts and identification for accuracy.
9. Make a specific list of all assets owned in your name only and one of all those owned jointly with others. Be specific and check this list annually.
10. Prepare a will if you do not want to use the in testate law to determine who will receive your property when you are gone.
11. Check health, life, liability and property insurance each year. Be sure all personal information is correct. Keep copies in a safe place.
12. Make a list of all credit account numbers and mailing addresses to reach all your creditors in an emergency.

    This list will provide a rough outline of where to begin. Each individual must review his/her own facts and circumstances to determine any additional items needed to be on the list. The primary goal is for the individual to be prepared in case something unexpected happens. Failure to take any action at all creates opportunity for worry about the future and increases the chances of making mistakes when actual emergencies or life events arise. Sooner or later, everyone has to deal with an emergency in life, so be prepared. Trying to avoid a crisis when unprepared and under stress is the worst position to be in.
    Creditors also like consumers to use credit because they do not have to handle cash. For creditors, the use of credit has many of the same advantages as for consumers. Frequently, the use of credit is often cheaper and faster to work electronically than using hard currency. Creditors also like the fact they do not have to stop to check credit status for every transaction. Almost half of consumer installment credit is through credit card accounts, and the percentage is growing rapidly. Some economic experts are already predicting the success of the cashless society. It is

not surprising that the universal bank credit card became popular in the early days of the social revolution. One woman's comment emphasizes the importance of a credit line:

> *I had to use a cash advance on my account to help with the down payment on a car. A male or female on his/her own may not have extra money. My paycheck is spent before I get it. My credit card is absolutely necessary just for me to survive between paychecks. Thank goodness I can use my credit card at the grocery store.*

Credit is important, but it can also be dangerous. The dangers to the inexperienced is well known, so it must be used maturely. Too often people carry too large a debt obligation on open accounts accessed by credit cards. Such a practice is a misuse of credit. The best use for credit is for emergencies and not as a means to finance an unrealistic life style. Over extension of credit as a means to maintain a desired life style overrides common sense. The best use of credit cards is to pay off the balance on a monthly basis to avoid interest payments and compounded charges.

The Equal Credit Opportunity Act (ECOA) is the law that gave females equal access to credit. This law is the single most important law created during the social revolution. However, the original bias that led to the passage of ECOA was limited to married women. ECOA was not passed until the mid 1970's, well into the social revolution and after the end of the American Dark Ages. This law was essential because the original credit bias against married women was so powerful, it virtually denied them the ability to obtain credit in their own names at one of the most important times in our history. The practice that created the bias can be best explained in terms of an example:

> *James T. Rowe, who is married to Jane Rowe, needs a loan to buy farm equipment to run a farm he owns down the street from their home. The farm is owned in his name only and was inherited from his father. He applies for credit to be used to finance the purchase of the equipment. He is approved for the loan in his own name. The loan officer asks him what day he and his wife can come in for the loan closing since they will both be required to sign all the loan documents.*
>
> *Since the loan is to be secured by the farm equipment, the documents consist of a note, which is the promise to repay the amount due and the terms of the repayment obligation, the required disclosure*

statements, and a Uniform Commercial Code Financing statement to create a first lien on the equipment.

At closing both James Rowe, and his wife, Jane, sign all the documents requested by the lender.

To understand this innocent appearing form of discrimination, carefully review exactly what happened. In the example, James purchased the equipment in his name only. Jane was not involved in the purchase transaction. James applied for a loan to finance the new equipment in his name only. Jane did not apply for the loan. James was approved for the loan in his name only. Jane was not needed to obtain the loan in any way. However, the lender required Jane to sign all the documents at closing. The questions are why was she required to sign the documents in a transaction where she was not a party, and what were the consequences to her when she did?

The answer to the first question is that the only tie for her to the transaction is that she is married to James. She was required to obligate herself to repay the debt solely because of the condition of marriage. If she were not married to James, she would not have been required to sign any documentation whatsoever. This practice of requiring the spouse of an approved applicant to sign the loan documents as an obligor with full responsibility to repay the debt was customary throughout the American Dark Ages. Surprisingly, the required joinder of a spouse to all credit documents had no foundation in legal practice. The practice was simply adopted because of the underlying myths in our culture.

Most lenders, when asked why they had such a requirement, could only explain that this was the way they had always done business. Surprisingly, lenders could not provide a more definitive explanation for their requirements. However, the answer is quite simple. Lenders were acting in accord with our culture and the pictures we carry in our subconscious that define who we are. On marriage, a wife merges into and becomes a part of her husband, so if he is required to sign, so must she as a part of him. If you look at the practice in light of the old story, understanding the custom becomes clear.

Before ECOA, our society was strictly old culture, and everyone lived by internal old culture images and behaved automatically according to the cultural myths, without thinking. The first image in the old culture was the merger of the female back into the male through the myth where poor Adam was made whole again. Acting out this image, Jane Smith became Mrs. James T. Rowe. She simply disappeared as a separate individual.

Therefore, since she was now a part of James, she was required to sign the closing documents, even financially she had become part of her husband.

The practice seemed so innocent that it prevailed generation after generation, and no one ever challenged it. Besides, both men and women were old culture, so simply, no one questioned the net effect of the practice. However, with the arrival of the social revolution, transitional females began to reject the old culture images and sought to obtain credit on their own. Whether they were unmarried, married, or had divorced poor Adam and started life on their own, they began to build a financial status of their own. The key element of the social revolution was that significant numbers of married women began to see themselves as unique human beings, separate from their husbands.

Before ECOA, if a woman, married or divorced, decided to buy a car on her own in her own name using her own funds, she discovered that she could not qualify for the loan for the following reasons:

> She already had too much debt where she was obligated to pay loans she had signed with her husband.
>
> If joint loan history was poor, her credit rating was affected and she did not qualify for a new loan.
>
> If the loan was paid off according to its terms, she could not use it as a credit reference because the loan was only indexed in her husband's name.
>
> Sometimes, even if the loan was repaid, the lender would deny the use of the payment history as a reference because the loan was actually paid by her husband.

The net result was that a married woman had full responsibility for repayment of her husband's loans, while she received none of the benefits toward her credit history. As long as our society was old culture, the unfairness of the practice was unseen. When the revolution brought in the concept that married women were actually separate, individual human beings, the discriminatory nature of the practice became obvious. The anti-female economic prejudice is illustrated by an extension of the example:

> *Jane Rowe inherited several thousand dollars from her uncle. When the equipment loan was not paid and she had divorced James T. Rowe, the lender sued her on her promise to pay the debt since*

she signed the note. In the end, the lender obtained a judgment against her and she lost her property to the farm equipment lender.

Many women found their credit ratings ruined by their husband's poor credit rating or default before they ever had a need to use credit for themselves. In the days before ECOA, women assisted in maintaining the bias because they too thought of themselves as part of their husbands. They also accepted the status quo and made no objection to the practice. Thus the bias was not one by men against women, but men and women created a bias against women through the acceptance of their culture. This acceptance of the practice resulted in the creation of the bias and caused repression of females.

The Equal Credit Opportunity Act [ECOA] was originally designed to remove this credit bias against married women. However, ECOA was also drafted and expanded to cover all discrimination based on sex and marital status. As a result, ECOA became the first law acting directly to counter the old culture myth of marriage as the merger of the female back into the male. The law has been expanded to prohibit discrimination against many classifications other than sex and marital status. However, the original focus is just as important today as it was back years ago.

Every bank or applicable financial institution is required by law to post, in a prominent place, a notice substantially similar to the following:

It shall be unlawful for any creditor to discriminate against any applicant, with respect to any aspect of a credit transaction-
(1) on the basis of race, color, religion, national origin, sex, marital status, age (provided the applicant has the capacity to enter into a binding contract);
(2) because all or a part of the applicant's income derives from any public assistance program; or
(3) because the applicant has in good faith exercised any right under The Consumer Credit Protection Act.

This brief notice is the foundation of ECOA. Yet, today few consumers even know it exists or are aware of its deep reaching effects. This notice prohibits the bias against married women. The elimination of this bias may have been the initial motivator in getting ECOA passed into law, but the law now covers all discrimination based on sex and marital status as well as all the other listed categories. Even though

ECOA was passed back in the 1970's, it remains the law of the land to this day. To read the actual Act, it may be found in the United States Code Annotated under Title 15 Section 1691 in the local library reference section. Regulation B, which consists of the regulation implementing the law, can be obtained through The Federal Reserve Board in Washington, D.C. if the local library or a neighborhood creditor does not have a copy.

The rest of this law is important also. However, the focus of this text is limited to the original law that deals with discrimination based on sex and marital status. There are some terms under ECOA that aid in understanding how it works:

> **Applicant**: Any person who applies to a creditor directly for an extension, renewal, or continuation of credit, or applies to a creditor indirectly by use of an existing credit plan for an amount exceeding a previously established credit limit. See Title 15 Section 1691 a. (a).

Remember, the law is limited. The law only applies to credit transactions, not with other kinds of discrimination. Simply stated, if a transaction does not meet the definitions stated in the law, ECOA does not apply. The law applies to persons who are creditors.

> **Creditor**: Any person who regularly extends, renews, or continues credit; or any assignee of an original creditor who participates in the decision to extend, renew, or continue credit. See Title 15 Section 1691 a.(e).

What is important here is that the law does not regulate anyone other than creditors. In short, the law only protects applicants against discrimination by creditors in all aspects of a credit transaction. ECOA was originally passed to make the anti-female implications of the original bias illegal where females could not gain access to credit on their own. ECOA can be studied by looking at how the old culture images denied women access to credit. Society unconsciously had to make poor Adam whole again, and merged the female into the male on marriage, thus reducing her to a non-entity.

The plight of women lacking credit in the social revolution demanded action. ECOA was passed to outlaw the practices of the old culture that had the effect of creating discrimination against women for credit. Without understanding that ECOA was specifically designed to offset the old culture story of marriage as the merger of the female back into the male, ECOA and Regulation B are more difficult to understand.

While ECOA did place a number of obligations on creditors, the focus here is on how the law affects the consumer directly. The consumer will find it difficult to find a seminar or education course that covers ECOA. However, the law itself includes only the general provision of discrimination against applicants on a prohibited basis, so it is fairly straightforward. Regulation B is even more helpful because it itemizes some of the specific prohibitions. Regulation B demonstrates exactly how the bias was countered.

Some of the relevant provisions are set out as follows with citations to the exact part of the regulation included to facilitate easy reference to look them up:

> A creditor shall not refuse to allow an applicant to open or maintain an account in a birth given first name and a surname that is the applicant's birth-given surname, the spouse's surname or a combination surname. See Reg. B Section 202.7(b).

Notice that this provision precisely counters the prevailing old culture concept that on marriage, the female disappears and merges back into the male. In the American Dark Ages, this was a country of "Mrs. John Does," where the female gave up her identity. The way to counter the credit bias was to encourage both men and women to think of females as separate individual human beings. The best way to do that was to encourage the use of individual names not limited to those of their husbands. Allowing women to have the ability be financially separate from their husbands for credit purposes also had a powerful effect on the economy. This effect of encouraging women to see themselves as financially separate individuals further promoted the revolution as well as the economy.

> A creditor that furnishes credit information shall designate the account to reflect participation of both spouses if the applicant's spouse is permitted to use or is contractually liable on the account. See Reg. B Section 202.10 (a).

One of the most powerful aspects of the credit bias was that loan records before ECOA were only kept in the name of the husband, even though the wife was equally liable to repay the debt. This provision allowed women to use any loan for which she was legally liable as a credit reference. This provision also helped many women establish credit using loans that may actually have been paid by their husbands. On the other hand, if a person was legally liable to pay a loan, they had a right to use it as a credit reference. The danger of this provision is that a bad payment history on a loan where both spouses are liable will reflect on both credit ratings.

Offsetting this danger is the fact that women began to ask themselves why they were obligating themselves to repay debts that belonged only to their husbands. If they would gain no benefit from a loan, why should they agree to repay it and potentially damage their personal credit rating or risk losing their property? As women began to think of themselves as separate individual human beings different from their husbands, they went through a change in orientation that played a key role in the revolution.

> If a creditor furnishes credit information to a consumer-reporting agency, it must furnish the information in the name of each spouse, especially in the name of the spouse about whom the information is requested. See Reg. B Section 202. 10 (b) and (c).

This provision is simply an expansion of the previous one emphasizing the separate nature of credit ratings for individuals and the need to keep separate records for each party who is legally obligated to repay a loan. This provision directly affects the combination or joint accounts offered to married couples by many retail creditors.

> A creditor can only use the terms "married," "unmarried," or "separated," but the creditor can indicate that the term "unmarried" includes single, divorced and widowed persons. See Reg. B Section 202.5 (d).

This provision is sometimes called the anti-soap opera provision because it outlaws the old practice of using phrases such as the following:

> Jane Rowe, divorced and not since remarried.
> Jane Rowe, widow of John Rowe, deceased.
> Jane Rowe, divorced from William Rowe.

A creditor cannot require an individual to disclose marital status for credit application purposes. If approved by a lender, the lender can require a good first mortgage on any approved collateral for the loan. Marital status at the time of closing is a legitimate inquiry if a spouse has an interest in the property offered as collateral.

The following examples demonstrate violations of ECOA and Regulation B provisions. They provide a flavor for how the regulation is applied:

> A creditor states on the application form that if there are joint applicants, they must be related by blood or marriage.
>
> A creditor approves males and females for the same loan program, but offers different loan terms depending on sex and marital status.
>
> A creditor requires the guarantee by the husband of a loan application made solely by the wife before the creditor processes the loan or determines her credit rating.

A number of cases interpreting ECOA clearly state that the purpose of ECOA was to eradicate credit discrimination against women, especially married women. The cases pointed out that creditors traditionally refused to consider married women for individual credit. The intent of the law is to prohibit creditors from requiring the signature of an applicant's spouse in those cases where the applicant individually qualified under the creditor's standards for the loan requested. Thus ECOA has forced society to deal with the issue of what marriage means when the parties are legally recognized as equal human beings. A creditor can set a standard as to what constitutes a complete loan application. Until an application is completed, the creditor is under no obligation to take any action to process it, but the creditor does have to provide the appropriate notices under the law. See Reg. B Section 202.9 (c) (1).

If a husband and wife both submit a co-application, the creditor is totally justified in requiring both parties to sign all the loan documents because they are both voluntary parties to the transaction. The bias only arose when the wife did not volunteer to participate in the loan. If a woman fills in a loan application and uses a courtesy title such as "Mrs." followed by her husband's name, the creditor is not required to look for a more definitive name to find a credit history. In fact, creditors will avoid such inquiries because they would be a violation of ECOA. The use of "Mrs." is strictly old culture and is clear evidence that the woman sees herself as part of her husband. Since there is no combined credit rating for a married couple, the use of this designation does not help either the applicant or the creditor and only leads to confusion.

The best way for women to apply for credit is to decide what name to use for all financial transactions before filling out an application for credit. A creditor will always check credit only in the name submitted and precisely as written on the application. Always remember, the old culture images help understand the logic behind ECOA and regulation B. If ECOA teaches anything, ECOA encourages applicants to think cautiously before applying for credit.

The promissory note is evidence of the debt and the obligation to repay it. Those signing the note are the ones who are legally obligated to repay the indebtedness. Credit ratings are based in part on the payment history of the notes on which the borrower is liable as an obligor. Just remember, the execution of a mortgage is not a credit document if the signature is required solely to perfect the security interest in property used as collateral.

Property rights will be covered in more detail in subsequent chapters. A preliminary example follows to help explain the difference between an obligor on the note and a mortgagor where the lender requires a first lien under state law on all interests in the property used for collateral:

> *James Rowe is married to Diane Rowe. He applies for a purchase money mortgage to finance the purchase of a rental duplex in a state where they do not live. He is the only buyer on the contract. He is approved for the loan in his own name.*

James is the only one required to sign the note because he is both the only applicant and the only one required to repay the debt. He is the only one to sign the mortgage as long as his wife has no statutory interest in the property under the laws of the state where the land is located. Keep in mind, if James Rowe's credit is turned down as insufficient, and Diane volunteers to be a co-applicant, cosigner, or guarantor for the loan and the loan is then approved, she would be a required signatory on the note. However, the real question coming out of the revolution, is why would she be willing to sign the note as an obligor, cosigner or guarantor and assume liability for the payment of the debt if she obtains no benefit from the loan? Her decision can often be centered on whether the property is the family residence, and what ownership interest she has in the property.

Love and affection are sufficient legally to support a spouse signing as an obligor where the proceeds of the loan will go to the other spouse. However, the real issue of whether a spouse should do so at all if the loan does not benefit that spouse hinges on whether the spouse is old culture and sees herself as merged into and part of her husband, or whether she is transitional and sees herself as a separate individual person. To say it another way, the request of one spouse for the other to act as an obligor, cosigner or guarantor puts on the table what marriage means to the one asked to sign.

The threshold question for those in such circumstances is what property rights are being put at risk if the spouse agrees to sign? A second question is to ask is why is the second spouse asked to assume responsibility for a debt where there is no direct benefit? The key to being aware of the dangers of the influence of old culture habits is the recognition of the need to ask questions to avoid acting automatically without thinking.

Of course, the answers depend on many factors, including personal and financial circumstances, the laws of the state, the details involved in the transaction, and most of all what marriage means to the parties involved. The emphasis here on applicants, approved borrowers and required signatures for those who have an interest in the property is due to the issues that come up in thousands of transactions across this country every day, but are overlooked by those who are not aware of the consequences of their actions. As a part of the journey to awareness, it is imperative to know the implications of what is being signed and why. Only the person signing a document can decide how to handle a spouse's request to be an applicant or a cosigner or even just sign a first mortgage for security purposes. Remember that the same issues exist in both directions, when one spouse asks the other to sign a document. Why is that spouse asking the other to sign? What are the consequences to each individual if they consent to do so?

These types of requests always justify an analysis of what marriage means to each spouse. The degree to which a person submits their property interest to the desires of the other spouse depends on the answers of what marriage means to them. If asked to sign a mortgage to bind an interest in the family home owned by one spouse alone, and the other spouse believes in supporting the efforts of the other spouse without question, that spouse may decide to sign without further inquiry. On the other hand, a transitional may want to be sure that their individual interests are protected in the event of a default in the loan by the other spouse.

A loan application may be denied due to insufficient credit or insufficient security. What is really at risk is how the parties define their marriage. Whether a current or subsequent marriage fails, credit ratings belong to individuals and is of value at all times. Most individuals will need to use their credit at some time sooner or later, no matter what happens to his/her marital status. Individuals who are caught in their own personal struggle as to what marriage means to them are often confused about their identity as separate unique human beings from their spouse. As long as the old culture images lie deep within the psyche of individuals in society, clashes between its images and rights under ECOA will remain with us and in society as well.

ECOA is not a law that expressly grants rights to those discriminated against. Rather, it is a law that prohibits creditors from doing certain things that, if not followed, would result in prohibited discrimination. This law has been in effect since the 1970's, so awareness and compliance are high. Credit agencies have educational programs to be sure their personnel know the law and Regulation B. As a result, creditors follow its provisions regardless of the personal biases and prejudices of their employees. For example:

> *I am an unmarried female. I sell stationary and other paper products to banks and other creditors. I have to call on a certain bank manager on a regular basis. Every time I make a sales call he makes me feel very uncomfortable. He spends most of our meeting telling me about his wife and kids. He has pictures of them on his desk and credenza that he shows to me every time I visit him. I wish ECOA protected me so I didn't have to put up with what I feel is an attempt to make me feel uncomfortable because I am unmarried and I do not have a family.*

ECOA does not protect her from his behavior. ECOA only protects applicants for credit from discrimination by creditors. ECOA provides no protection from direct or indirect harassment or discrimination in any other way. Even though she is calling on creditors, she is likely to encounter many old culture people. Pictures on the credenza or desk can be signs of an old culture person or pictures may be in the office merely to remind the occupant of their family. In some cases, family pictures may actually be a sign that the person is insecure about their family relationships. The old culture individual often needs the visual reinforcement that they have made poor Adam whole again and are living life in accordance with the old culture images. The pictures demonstrate that he or she has the old culture possessions consisting of a spouse and children and is complying with the lifestyle dictated by internal images. The pictures help them survive the difficult days dealing with issues that do not allow behavior to conform with the internal self-image. Thus, family pictures often serve a therapeutic and reinforcement purpose for the individual.

However, family pictures can be more than internal reinforcement. They may act as an announcement to others that the person who occupies the office is old culture. When a visitor is also old culture, they can discuss their families at great length. This activity provides needed reinforcement of their social orientation. On the other hand, when an unmarried person visits the old culture person, sharing pictures may be done for one or a combination of several other reasons. First, old culture people usually do not see other people as different from themselves. For this reason, they may be unaware that another person may have a totally different social or cultural orientation. Thus, the old culture person treats everyone exactly the same way. They are simply proud of their family.

Second, the old culture person usually has a deep-seated need to assure that poor Adam has been made whole again. Any unmarried person is fair game in an effort to encourage them towards the virtues of marriage. Third, others may serve as an escape for the old culture person's need to avoid thinking about work, which to them is dull and boring.

The young woman in the above example should not feel singled out by the old culture person's behavior. A similar complaint was expressed by a male calling on an old culture male who had pictures of his family in his office and liked to spend time in every meeting discussing his family. The man who was complaining had lost his wife and small son in an automobile accident. Old culture people are often oblivious to the needs and feelings of others.

Family pictures in the office setting are not the only warnings of an old culture orientation. Pictures of boats, cars, houses, or vacation trips may also act as warnings of an old culture orientation. A good rule of thumb to follow is that if more than twenty percent of your conversation in a business meeting dwells on any of the following topics the occupant of the office is old culture:

1. Family
2. Sports
3. Hobbies
4. Vacations
5. Retirement

There is nothing wrong with any of these topics, but they are not relevant in a business conversation, except maybe to briefly open or close the meeting. The person who dwells on these topics in the business environment is telling you that they are working at a job not a career, and they would rather be somewhere else. Often they are trapped in their present position by an old culture orientation. The only tactic to use when the business conversation stalls on irrelevant topics is to politely steer the conversation to the subject of the meeting. Meetings in the office should be focused on the business purpose at hand. However, the old culture thinking is still with us, and transitional people will have to handle situations with old culture people who do not see the world the same way they do.

Transitional people are less likely to have personal pictures in the office because they have strong personal relationships where all people are seen as unique human beings. They do not need photographs as props or devices to reinforce their relationships. More importantly, they do not intrude in the personal lives of others and do not expect or desire others to interfere in theirs. They see the work environment as limited to work related functions, and they respect the time requirements of business visitors and associates. They keep their office environment and conversations focused on business purposes for which it exists.

Although the young woman in the example felt uneasy, there was no ECOA violation in the banker's behavior. The real problem is that the underlying old culture thinking is still prevalent in the general population. Clashes with ECOA result because the general public is not prohibited from the same activities as creditors. The following example shows how the old culture exists in the public and how ECOA can be misunderstood:

> *I'm a female manager of a small branch of a bank. We have an elderly woman customer who comes in quite frequently. She refuses to deal with me. I can only communicate with her through our part time male teller. She claims ECOA gives her the right to talk to the man in charge.*

The elderly customer is confused about ECOA. ECOA does not give her the right to select the gender of the person she contacts at the lending institution or even the right to meet with a person in a particular position. ECOA only prohibits creditors from discriminating on a prohibited basis in any aspect of a credit transaction. The example shows how the public usually has little actual knowledge of the law, and how old culture females are one of the major problems faced by transitional women.

There is no public training on ECOA or Regulation B, so there is no awareness of a need to change old attitudes and deeply set habits and thinking concerning credit issues for the public. To the extent the public unconsciously carries the old culture images, clashes with ECOA will continue into the future.

One of the more common conflicts faced by merchants on a fairly regular basis, occurs when the wife of an account holder proposes using a credit card belonging to her spouse to purchase items on her own. When she is refused the use of the card because she is not a signatory and has not been authorized to use the card, her response often is:

> *I am insulted. I have been married to this man for the last fifteen years. I cannot believe you are denying me the right to use his card. Fifteen years of marriage is long enough to give me the right to use his account. I want to see a manager and file a complaint.*

If she does not have her own account, then she must be an authorized signatory on his account. In this case, she should have her own card giving her a right to access his account. If all she has is his card, and she is not a signatory on his account, she has no right to use the card she has tendered. Even though this situation seems straightforward, it continues to occur on a regular basis across this country. Merchants continue to induce the homemaker spouse to open her own account in her name. If unsuccessful, they try to obtain authorization from the husband to allow her to have her own credit card to access his account. In either case, the merchant has to endure her wrath for the refusal to allow her to use her husband's card. The problem is that the woman who offers her husband's credit card is strictly old culture, and she thinks of herself as part of her husband right out of the old story, where marriage has merged her back into poor Adam to make him whole again. If she were transitional, she would have obtained her own account when she first realized she was a separate person.

To the old culture wife, marriage has made her part of Adam with no identity of her own. Thus, there is no reason in her mind why she should not be able to use his card, and she will be leery of any offer by the merchant to open a new account in her own name, separate from her husband. Merchants are aware of this resistance so they usually offer a number of economic incentives for the wife to open a new account in her name only. The merchant will often try economic inducements to customers to overcome resistance for opening an account in her name only.

Of course, another reason she does not already have a credit account of her own is that her old culture husband does not see her as a separate person. The husband's old culture concept of marriage as the merger of married people into one with the male the survivor is the reason they have only one account, and one card in his name only. The husband often sees a second account in his wife's name as a threat to his old culture sense of personal identity. Having a spouse with financial independence would conflict with his internal image of himself as the knight. A separate account in her name would require him to recognize her as an equal human being, something an old culture male cannot accept.

For these reasons, the merchant will try to induce the wife to open a new account on her own without contacting her husband for permission. The merchant will often open a separate account in her name only with a low credit approval limit at least until a payment history is established. The merchant knows that over time, the wife who has a separate account means the wife will spend more than she otherwise would. For this economic reason, the merchant will try to induce the woman to sign up for her own account while she is on the sales floor and has no chance to discuss the matter with her husband. The merchant is very aware that the old culture male is not likely to approve the separate account. The economic incentives often sway the old culture wife to open her own account in spite of her misgivings. Sometimes an account in her own name has the effect of opening her mind to the fact she is a separate person and starts her on the way to becoming transitional- a big step for her.

On the other hand, the merchant's life is not easy because the old culture wife often identifies herself only as "Mrs." followed by her husband's name. The merchant must induce her to volunteer a full name for their account records. The tight restrictions of ECOA prohibit the creditor from asking about sex or marital status so the creditor has a difficult burden if it wants more than the "Mrs." designation on the account. All applicants must provide a full formal name voluntarily for the application to be acceptable. The danger of the use of "Mrs. James Rowe" on the application is that after the death of the husband or after divorce the designation creates confusion. This confusion is compounded today especially after divorce when he remarries and there is a new person with this same designation. The original woman who used "Mrs. James Rowe," once divorced, will have trouble using the account as a credit reference or maintain it on her own because of the inability to specifically identify the person owning the account. Because of this potential confusion, each woman must use her full name at all times regardless of marital status.

ECOA only affects creditors by prohibiting discrimination in all aspects of a credit transaction. ECOA does not regulate anyone else in any way, so old culture prejudice still permeates our society. Just because the merchant and creditor must deal with the general public, they are often confused over exactly who the applicant is when the applicant has not provided a clear disclosure of his/her identity.

An example of such confusion occurs when a husband applies for a home improvement loan and the creditor discovers that the real estate is rental property owned solely by the wife. In this case, the husband has no interest in the property under state law. Since the proceeds of the loan are restricted to the costs of the improvements, the husband has no personal economic interest in the loan whatsoever. In this case, the husband is confused as to his role in applying to the creditor. His confusion leaves the creditor uncertain as to the role of the husband. If the husband insists on making an application, the creditor would have to accept it and subsequently reject the loan for inadequate security since the property is not in his name. In the given example, the correct loan applicant is the wife since she owns the property in her own name and the loan proceeds benefit her alone. Often the only reason the husband is making the application is that he thinks of himself as the male in the old culture picture of the knight who owns the castle. In the old culture image, princesses do not own castles or apply for loans.

Often, creditors also create the very confusion they complain about. For example, some creditors will allow the husband to open an account in his name and the wife to open an account in her name. Then they allow the couple to open an account in both names under what they will often label a joint account. The combined, joint account is the merchant's expression of the old culture concept of the couple as one by virtue of marriage. However, there is no such thing as a separate credit identity for a married couple. Thus, the creditor must still maintain credit information under both names separately since both spouses are liable for the joint account. Unfortunately, this third account concept does have the effect of confusing applicants about the difference between their individual identities and what they perceive as their combined existence as a married couple.

There are limitless examples in our society where there is economic preference given to married couples over those who are unmarried. These business practices are expressions of the old culture concept of the merger of the male and female together as one through marriage. From the old culture merchant's viewpoint, the couple is one and the unmarried person is one so the merchant does not recognize the bias that the unmarried transitional person feels. Our society is permeated with marital incentive programs showing the old culture is alive and well, even though we are several years into the Transition. Rarely, if ever, do you see an incentive program for the single person, particularly in the travel and vacation industry where singles pay an additional fee when they do not have a traveling companion.

Lack of understanding of the conflict of culture with ECOA can create confusion that often results in a loss of protected rights. For example:

> *Ever since my husband died, I just assumed that my account at the department store was cancelled. I destroyed my card and never used the account again.*

If the account was his account and she only had the use of his account through a duplicate or separate card printed in her name, she is right. Of course, such an account is strictly an expression of the old culture concept of the wife merging back into the husband. However, in such cases it is appropriate to close his account on his death. On the other hand, if the account she had was in her own name, the merchant cannot legally close it on the death of her husband. Such an act would be a violation of ECOA. On the death of her spouse, she would need an account in her own name more than ever before. Closing the account at his death would be a mistake if she needed the use of such an account. Even if there were only one account in his name, she would be wise to apply for an account in her name as soon as possible. If access to his account was convenient, a new one in her name would be even more useful now that he is gone. ECOA prevents cancellation of the account of a spouse on the death of the other spouse if the accounts are separate and not guaranteed by the deceased spouse.

Another case where confusion results in giving up rights protected under ECOA is illustrated by the following example:

> *I felt awkward in saying it, but my husband had early symptoms of memory loss. He paid his account with the department store only when he remembered. Sometimes he let it go for months. Finally, I was so embarrassed I cancelled my account. In fact, I threw the card away. The account was paid in full, but I'm sure they cancelled me when he was seriously delinquent. I didn't want to receive any threatening phone calls.*

If she has a separate account that is not guaranteed by her husband, the creditor cannot cancel her account because of the adverse credit rating or delinquent status of her husband's account. In the above example, his credit rating may be ruined but hers is not.

Both of these examples show how the old culture image of married people as one influence the decisions of people who are not aware of the provisions of ECOA that protect them against the power of culture. In both cases, credit accounts were erroneously given up at the very time when they may have been important, and both were given up because of old culture thinking. ECOA offers limited but important legal counters to old culture habits and traditions for those who are aware of the opportunities they offer.

CHAPTER SIX: PROPERTY OWNERSHIP

Throughout our lives, people continually deal with property from daily household purchases to bank accounts, automobiles, and the most important, a home. There is little value in knowing the influence of culture on women's rights concerning credit unless one also knows the influence of culture on property ownership. The major reason people need credit is to acquire property, usually without the immediate ability to pay for it. Thus, property and credit are interrelated. Studying one without spending time on the other is not possible. The old culture story that incorporates the concept of the merger of the male and female together as one through marriage is deeply interwoven into the ownership of property much as in the area of credit before the adoption of ECOA.

However, similar protections against the influence of culture applicable to property ownership are not covered by ECOA. Little federal regulation of property rights exists outside certain securities and environmental regulations. The laws governing property rights are determined by individual states. Instead of fighting culture, most states actually adopt culture into the options available for property ownership. The laws affecting property ownership vary on a state-by-state basis. There are some common ways culture can trap the unwary when dealing with the different types of property ownership.

Property is divided into two types, personal property and real estate. The danger presented by the old culture images varies somewhat depending on which classification applies to the subject property. Without going into great detail here, there is also a hybrid type of property called "fixtures." Fixtures consist of personal property that becomes attached to and a part of real estate to the extent title to fixtures is transferred with the real estate. However, fixtures are purchased as personal property, and, from an awareness standpoint, they should be classified as such because the old culture bias may appear in the same way. When dealing with personal property, be careful how ownership or title is held, and in what name(s). Thus, when dealing with personal property, the old culture danger most often comes not from others, but from within the owner(s) or purchaser(s) themselves. The transfer of title that takes place when personal property becomes affixed to real estate to the extent it becomes part of the real property creates the danger. For example:

> *Richard Rowe and Roxanne Rowe own their home together (Joint ownership is covered in subsequent chapters). Roxanne purchases a heating-air conditioning unit and uses her personal credit line to pay for the unit. Richard is not a party to this account. On installation, the unit becomes part of the property. Although owned by both as co-owners, only Roxanne has the legal obligation to pay the indebtedness on her account.*

The issue becomes more dramatic if Richard owns the property in his name only, and even more so if they are not married. Such incidents occur many times over in real life today. In addition, people may try to influence how to title property by making suggestions to you. For example:

1. Should you add your husband on the deed?
2. Why don't you leave your wife off the title?
3. Since you are married, shouldn't you put title in your husband's name?
4. Don't you think married people should hold title together?

Do not underestimate the efforts of others to influence how to title your personal property. However, they may simply be expressing old culture biases. Be sure to keep in mind their efforts remain no more than suggestions. The ultimate decision is always totally in the hands of the purchaser/owner. Be aware of the attempt of outsiders to influence the actions of others to conform to their old culture social orientation. However, others are not the primary danger in personal property transactions.

In general, personal property is titled under the laws of the state where the property is first sold to the general public. Airplanes, automobiles, and boats and a few other items have very specific laws on title documentation and lien registration. For other personal property, the Uniform Commercial Code has been adopted by most states to unify the process of creating liens, but ownership of these items is usually limited to receipts and bills of sale with no central form of title registration. However, the influence of culture on ownership of personal property primarily comes from the social orientation of the person buying the property. Thus, the dangers of concern arise from within the purchaser rather than from outsiders.

Fortunately, the party preparing the ownership documentation for personal property is usually disinterested and passive. For example, when opening a bank checking or savings account or purchasing a certificate of deposit, the bank will provide documents that require the names and options available for multiple owners. Bank personnel will wait for the customer to fill in the forms. While the old culture orientation of an individual employees may cause some personnel to make recommendations, only the depositor(s)/owner(s) are legally allowed to make the decision of who the documented owners are. Employees will only follow the written instructions provided on the forms filled out and filed with them.

If questions about the ownership options available arises, the bank employees will refer the customer to seek the advise of their own attorney, because commercial institutions cannot give legal advice. Only an attorney can legally advise the depositor on the legalities of the account and ownership. In many cases, the bank application form provides all options for the applicant to list the names to be on the account and check off the type of ownership desired. However, the answer to what marriage means to the applicant is interwoven into the ownership of personal property. For example:

> Mary Smith is engaged to be married. She has expensive living room furniture that she has just paid off. She and her fiancé agree that her furniture is more suitable than his for their new home. The issue for her is who owns the furniture when they move in together.

Should Mary transfer ownership of the furniture to her husband as the survivor by merger? Should she transfer ownership into both names together as one? Should she continue to own the furniture and simply allow it to be used in the marital home as long as they live together? These questions are important and will become serious issues if the couple splits up before marriage or divorces after the wedding. A simple bill of sale or written acknowledgement of transfer of ownership is all that is needed to prove any change in title, so the issue of ownership of personal property of low value brought into a marriage is often seen as unimportant. However when marriages fail, personal property of nominal value often becomes the primary area of contention in the divorce proceedings. How the parties define marriage will determine how title and ownership to property is held during the marriage. The influence of old culture thinking will impact on the definition of the marriage and ownership of property acquired before and during the marriage. For this reason, awareness of social orientation of the individuals involved becomes extremely important when dealing with personal property.

In the fable story image, the knight is the owner of the castle, and it remains in his name forever. In the real world, the ultimate question about the castle on the distant hill is who owns it now; what can the owner do with it; what does the influence of marriage and divorce have on ownership; and what happens to title when the owner dies. The most important asset anyone will ever own is a home, the castle in the image of the knight. For the home to truly be *the castle,* one must have, at least, a rudimentary understanding of the basic real estate concepts. Within the selection of the ownership options, old culture thinking can influence one to take action that is not in his or her best interests. When purchasing a condominium unit, an attached townhouse, or a single family residence, the dangers of old culture thinking loom over the decisions to be made and only awareness can save the purchaser from the negative influence of culture.

The old culture danger comes not just from within the individual, but from others, specifically those who prepare the documentation or closely related to the purchaser. The primary danger here is likely to be in assuming these third parties are disinterested, when, in fact, they will often make assumptions that actually determine the nature of the estate between the buyers. The problem is that these third party players often act automatically without discussing the options available with the buyer. Yet, their actions will control how title is held. There is a double concern here. In addition to the possible influence of the old culture from within, the buyer must also be alert for the influence of these service providers. As a result, the buyer must actively participate in the process of document preparation by affirmatively stating how they are to be titled and by checking all the closing documents before signing them to avoid any cultural bias coming from both internal and external sources.

The only way to avoid the pitfalls of old culture thinking in real estate ownership is to increase knowledge of property rights by reading about the applicable state laws, and by seeking qualified legal advice. Remember, one must be alert to the influence of old culture biases and how they affect the decision making process that controls the ownership of real estate. The important point is that no one else is going to look out for the buyer except the buyer. Even if an attorney is retained, be sure they are aware of what is desired. The power of old culture thinking affects everyone dealing with real estate. Also, remember that attorneys are not immune from the power of old culture thinking.

The ownership and lien laws concerning real estate are determined by the state where the property is located since real estate cannot be moved. Property laws address three issues: (1) how property is described, (2) how property is titled, including the interrelationship between the owners, and (3) how creditors who loan the money used to buy the property can perfect a lien to secure their loan. To maintain the focus on increasing awareness of the old culture dangers, the comments here are general. For the specifics refer to an attorney who practices real estate law in the state where the property is located. Thus, consult an attorney to answer specific questions regarding real estate and for advice and assistance in making personal and financial decisions regarding real estate. Knowing the applicable state laws for property ownership, especially for real property, is paramount.

The following chapters provide a brief overview of the general ownership concepts involved and include the most common ways to hold title to real estate. (Again, for specifics, check with an attorney in the state where the property is titled.) These chapters will address the primary way old culture thinking is likely to influence the various types of ownership. Remember that the greatest danger of old culture thinking is to assume one knows the answers to questions about title to property instead of seeking appropriate legal advice. All too often individuals assume that what they may have learned about the laws of one state will automatically apply to a neighboring state. This is a common but erroneous assumption to avoid. The following example interweaves property ownership and credit:

> *Robert Lowe visits a merchant who has a room of furniture that Robert has decided he wants to purchase. The merchant has a price of $2,000.00 but is willing to discount the price ten percent if Robert buys the merchandise on the date of the sale. Robert does not have the cash, and the merchant is unable to extend credit. The merchant will take a check but Robert does not have sufficient funds in his account to cover a check.*
>
> *Robert offers a universal bank credit card the merchant is willing to accept because the credit card company pays the merchant and extends credit to Robert.*
>
> *However Robert's credit limit on his account is only $1,000.00. The creditor tells Robert that if he owns his own home, they would*

> *consider a second mortgage on the property as long as the total debt on the property did not exceed 80% of the appraised value of the property.*
>
> *Robert rents and does not own any real estate, thus he is limited to his existing unsecured credit line because he has no security he can offer to justify a higher extension of credit. As a result, he is unable to buy the merchandise.*

What separates our country from much of the third world is our system of property description, ownership, and lien rights. Without these financial vehicles we would have to spend many years saving enough money to buy a car, furniture or a home. No one would loan us money to buy on credit if we could not describe the property; prove that we own it; or provide adequate security to a creditor to justify a loan.

In the United States, a creditor is encouraged to make loans because they have reason to feel secure in their investment. The creditor is protected under our system of ownership if the borrower does not pay. Coupled with the ability to use our system of credit ratings to evaluate risk, creditors can make an intelligent analysis of the risk versus the return on the money they lend. Everyone is protected, except the owner has no law to protect against the old culture bias that can put ownership at risk. An awareness of how to avoid being caught up in old culture dangers is important to economic survival and peace of mind today.

The primary old culture danger comes from the concept that married people are one and are not separate individuals. The private ownership of property becomes lost in this old culture thinking where the bias in favor of ownership together or in the name of the husband clouds the concept of individual ownership. To protect one's self from this old culture danger is to develop an awareness of property rights for items the individual owns. Individuals are advised to prepare and maintain a list of all property owned, whether young or old, male or female, married or unmarried.

This list should include all property owned individually or with others. Some items are easy to describe such as real estate, and automobiles, but other items such as coin collections, jewelry, antiques, and furniture can be more difficult. The only guideline is to be as precise and thorough as possible. Many insurance companies recommend video taping personal property. The key is to be able to identify one's property separate from any one else's. The more details included, the better. Once the list is compiled, sign the list and have the signature notarized showing the date when the list was effective. In addition to this asset list, review the desires for distribution of property if something happens to the owner. If the state inheritance laws do not meet your needs, you must use a will. Be sure to review personal and financial situations and personal goals with an attorney so personal interests are properly addressed. Have an attorney review the will to be sure it is properly drafted and executed. This will ensure it will be effective in the jurisdiction where it is to be probated. To be even more cautious, filing a current copy of one's will with the Probate Court where it will be processed while alive ensures that nothing will cause any problems after death. There have been cases where the original will has been lost, causing increased anguish and costs to the survivors. The following are a few minimal recommendations to help reduce the chances of being caught in any of the property ownership pitfalls:

1. Let relatives and significant others know where copies of your list are.
2. Keep one copy in the same location as your will.
3. Provide copies of your list to your insurance agent and underwriter. Keep a copy with every policy that insures any of the property on the list.
4. If your assets include stocks or bonds, then affix a broker's printout statement for the month you sign the list or prepare a list by hand.
5. Include the physical location where each item can be found if it is not kept in the same location as the list.
6. If there are holdings in stock that is in a private, unlisted company, be sure the company has been set up by an attorney and the certificates that represent the stock ownership are issued and preferably kept with the list.

Update the list periodically and recheck the will. Review both documents when changing ownership of any major capital items such as real estate or a major certificate of deposit, or if you relocate or move a substantial number of items owned. Estate attorneys will advise that one of their primary problems is to prepare an inventory of assets and locate all the property of the deceased person. Believe it or not, immediate family members are often not much help. One of the first steps to awareness is to know what one owns and keep an inventory in a safe place where others can find it if something happens to you. In addition to a periodic review of property and assets, some changes in life justify a more frequent review of the list of assets:

1. When adult children move in or out of your home.
2. After a divorce.
3. When adult children go through a divorce.
4. When entering a second or subsequent marriage.
5. When parents move in or out of your home.
6. When raising grandchildren.
7. When legally responsible for an unrelated adult or minor.
8. When facing changes in your personal life.
9. When anyone in the household faces changes in employment-income

These events are not exhaustive or by any means complete. They are intended only as a preliminary guide to emphasize the need to develop and maintain an accurate list of property and assets at all times. When reviewing an asset list, ask what the present and future situation is likely to be and whether ownership is consistent with long-range goals. The purpose of this activity is to determine if any ownership has been influenced by cultural bias without thought and without taking into account personal needs, interests and goals. Each individual is a unique person as to both financial circumstances and life goals. Any ownership that does not take these factors into account is not likely to produce the desired results. The ever-present danger is that culture may induce the individual to act automatically without thinking.

Another danger exists where failure to act in case some future event may or may not happen. For example:

I'll give them a ten thousand dollar certificate of deposit when and if they marry.
I'm going to wait until I think she is mature enough to manage the beach house on her own.
I'll deed the house to my daughter in her own name alone if they don't get married by the end of next year.
I'm not going to change my will right now. I'll wait until her divorce is final.

We are long past the days when the majority of residential real estate is occupied by the simple nuclear family consisting of both parents and their biological children. This old culture family has become a smaller percentage of the total number of residential households in this country every year. We must adjust our awareness so we take the new household structure into account when we consider property ownership. To do this, we must drop the old stereotypes that have dictated how we thought and acted back in the American Dark Ages. We are well into the Transition, and we need to adjust our thinking to the world around us to avoid being caught by customs and traditions that no longer apply.

If a daughter from a prior marriage moves back into the home with her small child, and it is unlikely that she will be able to survive out on her own, this fact needs to be taken into account in how to structure the ownership of the home and how it will be distributed if something happens to the owner. No one can predict the future, and nor can they totally predict how survivors will act when one is no longer here. The human dynamics between those who survive the deceased are likely to change when one dies. To sleep nights free of worry, one needs to prepare for the future as best to anticipate it in advance.

This completes our review of how old culture thinking affects property ownership. The following chapters review the specific types of ownership that are available and the old culture dangers that are associated with each specific type of ownership. This review should help identify the important issues in every real estate transaction. Hopefully, developing an awareness of the deep-seated cultural biases will aid in asking intelligent questions about the best way to own property in light of unique, personal and financial circumstances.

CHAPTER SEVEN: INDIVIDUAL OWNERSHIP

Why do we need to mention individual ownership?
Even with a heightened level of awareness of the merger of the female back into the male through marriage, the influence of the old culture may not be readily apparent with individual property ownership. Yet, the dangers lurk even here.

If property is held in an individual name, the owner has full dominion and control and can do as he/she wishes without taking into account the interests of anyone else. The problems begin when the time comes to sell the property, give it away, or include it in a will for transfer on death. Dangers lurk when others transfer property to the individual, so the pitfalls exist both when property is transferred to or from others.

This may seem obvious, but anyone can own property in his or her own name. The first old culture danger is that many people assume that property cannot be owned individually if one is married. Thus, the first rule to remember is that any one can own property in his or her individual name regardless of sex or marital status. In a great many states, that was not always true for females. Often, women had to go to court to prove they were capable of equal human status. Thankfully, that is no longer true today. The simple fact anyone can own property in their own name may appear straightforward, but there are many people who still believe that if married, they should only own property together, not individually. Such ideas are evidence of an old culture social orientation.

Let's look at a simple example of how the old culture concept that married people are one can influence ownership and create unintended consequences:

> *Mary Smith wanted to buy her daughter something special for her wedding, but she didn't know her daughter's fiancé very well. She wanted to protect her daughter just in case things didn't work out. Her plan was to give her daughter a certificate of deposit for $10,000.00. However, as the date of the wedding grew nearer, she had second thoughts. Perhaps she was doing the wrong thing. Perhaps, if she gave the gift to her daughter alone, that would be the factor that would drive them apart. Certainly, the divorce statistics were not in her daughter's favor. Shouldn't she be doing everything she could to promote the marriage? Ultimately, she decided to have both names on the certificate and gave it to them as a wedding gift.*
>
> *Later, at her daughter's divorce settlement, the court had the certificate split so that each marriage partner received half of the total principal.*

Mary's concerns initially had been good, but she yielded to the old culture concept that married people are one. Notice that she had choices. She could have held the money in her own name and kept it in reserve just in case her worst fears came true. She could also have had the certificate issued solely in her daughter's name and delivered it to her daughter privately.

Unfortunately for Mary and her daughter, these options yielded to the marriage ceremony as the celebration of the merger of the male and female together as one. The power of culture was greater than her initial instincts. Notice that her original intent was frustrated, not by others, but by her own thoughts and acts.

There are a multitude of books and movies where the parents of the bride make the gift of the deed to a home as a wedding present. Even on such a romantic and blissful occasion, reality can be much different than appears. For example:

> *What if, after the wedding the young bride opens the envelope containing the deed only to discover that the only name on the deed is her own? What should she do?*

Before deciding the answer to that question, consider another example:

> *What if the groom's parents made the gift of the deed to the new home, and the only name on the deed is their son, leaving the bride off all together? What should she do?*

Just to confuse matters before answering either question consider one more variation:

> *What if her parents made the gift of the deed, but they were strictly old culture and believed that not only were married people one, but the female merged back into the male. What if they executed the deed solely in the name of the husband, leaving her off altogether? What should she do?*

The one common element to all three examples is that the parents who executed the deed knew exactly what they were doing and gave up all interest in the property. Assuming the deed in each example had already been recorded, the bride cannot go back to the original owners. The second consideration is the laws of many states give some statutory rights to the non-owning spouse, especially when the property is the marital home. These laws vary from state by state so she must take time to discover the laws of the state where the property is located. Only when she knows the nature and extent of the legal rights that apply to her circumstances, she may answer the questions in the examples above.

If, in light of her particular circumstances, the statutory rights provided are acceptable to her, she might elect to do nothing. However, a non-owner spouse usually has a less secure position than the true owner, so doing nothing is often not an acceptable alternative. The answers to the questions posed in the three examples are not determined by state law, but by the personal and financial relationship between the individuals who are married to each other. The decision of what to do will be centered on the issue of what marriage means to each partner. The key to the solution will be what expectancy both persons have concerning the specific property. The issue raised in each example is simply what the marital relationship means to each spouse, and an understanding of their social orientation.

In the first example where the woman receives the property in her own name, she has the power to convey title to the property into both names. However, before she makes such a decision, she needs to think through her motivation since it may come from her internal image of herself as a married person under the old culture concept that male and female are one. The danger is that she could act automatically without thinking. She needs to ask herself what the full implications are of leaving title alone, and then consider the consequences if title is changed. The important point is that she needs to first stop and consider the alternatives thoroughly *before* she acts.

No one can tell her what to do. The answer for her depends on her social orientation, and her personal and financial circumstances and goals. Remember, the possibility exists that old culture thinking may be the source of her motivation. In the process of analysis, she also needs to consider the expectancy of her spouse, and that will be determined by whether he has an old culture orientation. The question for everyone dealing with situations like these is whether they think their spouse expects title to be in both names, and if so, why?

In the second example, the facts change, but the answer to the question is still centered around the woman's perception of herself as an old culture person where married people are merged as one and the female disappears into the male. When facing situations like the ones in the examples, the answer is determined by considering what each new spouse thinks marriage means to them. As a general statement, both the old culture male and female find it entirely appropriate to title the property in the name of the husband only, just as the parents did in conveying the property to the husband individually in the second two examples. Old culture people, at least unconsciously, see the female as merged into the male and accept male dominance including sole ownership of property as completely acceptable.

A transitional spouse will be sensitive to the concerns of the non-owner spouse, and most likely will have a deed prepared conveying title into both names even before the non-owner spouse asks about it. However, transitional marriages are not centered on the castle. Instead, they are focused on the interpersonal relationship. Property rights are just one subject included in a mutual understanding before marriage. Because transitionals are unique individuals, it is not possible to guess what any particular couple would agree on in every ownership situation. Since title in the last two examples is in the husband's name only, his perception of marriage prevails, not hers. The factors that determine what, if any, action is taken are his.

In the third example, the husband again owns the property alone. Does the young bride think the property should be owned in both names, even though the deed came from her parents, not his, and if so, why? There could actually be two reasons she reacts the way she does. First, she could be old culture and believe that married people are one, and all assets, especially including the marital home given as a gift at the wedding, should be in both names. She could also be transitional and believe that the wedding gift of the marital home should be owned equally by both spouses.

Her parents could be old culture, but she could believe in full equality and the marital home is often thought of as the most important element of this equality. If her husband dies owning the property in his name only, most state laws give her an interest in his estate whether or not he leaves her out of his will, but the issue of whether this statutory interest is satisfactory involves a complete analysis of their personal situations. If he dies insolvent, the castle may have to be sold to pay debts and the costs of administration of his estate.

The second part of the problem has nothing to do with her expectancy or motivation. Since the property is owned by her spouse alone, the real question is whether his social orientation is old culture or transitional. As in the second example, if he doesn't want to convey an interest to her, there's nothing she can do about it if she wants to keep her marriage intact. In most states, he is not free to deed or mortgage the property without her signature so her statutory interest is protected. Only if she has no legal interest in the property owned solely by her spouse is she at risk.

Remember, statutory rights are often limited and may depend on marriage and residency, in which case they may be lost, not just in the case of divorce, but even if she simply moves out of the marital home on her own. She must know the state law that applies in her situation before she takes any action. In any case, the motivation of her spouse will depend on his social orientation. If he is extremely old culture in orientation, he will feel property should be in his name only because she disappeared in the marriage ceremony. On the other hand, he could simply believe that married people are one, and conclude the marital home should be in both names.

If he is transitional, he will probably come to the conclusion that the property should be in both names. Because both parties are separate unique individuals, their home should be owned equally. The question, of course, remains the same. What does marriage mean to him? Many people in this country today don't know what marriage means to them. While this is not a fatal flaw when they are very young and have few assets, it can be crucial when they are older with small children and own property. It becomes even more important if they own assets and meet a potential new spouse.

The same issues arise in an example using a twist in the facts:

> *An uncle deeded a young woman a rental house in the city three years ago. She is now planning to get married in two months. At*

> *the time of the wedding, should she convey the property over in both names or leave it in her name?*

This example is a variation of the original three for a couple of reasons. In this case, the property is owned by the bride years in advance of the wedding, perhaps even well before the engagement. Secondly, the property is an investment asset and not the primary residence. Notice that, once again, the question cannot be answered unless the young woman understands what marriage means to her. The analysis of what marriage is depends on the degree to which the party is an old culture person. An extremely old culture person is one who not only believes that married people are one, but believes that the female merges back into the male. In such cases, old culture individuals with this orientation believe that the male should own all assets. The extreme old culture person is only comfortable with title vested in the husband alone. Never lose sight of the fact that either or both spouses can be old culture.

The moderate old culture person who only believes that married people are one without male superiority would be comfortable with title vested in both names. They believe people who marry should own things together as one, and should not own property as individuals separate from each other. A person who is transitional and outgrowing the old culture orientation would probably leave title alone. They would see marriage as a personal relationship between two individuals where property rights are simply a part of the individuals in the relationship. However, they are likely to have an advance agreement, i.e. a prenuptial agreement, covering all property no matter where or how obtained, so there is no misunderstanding about the ownership of existing or future property owned before, during, or after the relationship.

The television show where the pauper princesses compete for Prince Millibucks Charming is an excellent example of the most dangerous situation faced by many women. She may be easily swept away by the emotion of the moment when she meets the knight of her dreams who already owns a castle. Too often he will say:

> *Marry me and be my wife. All you have to do is move in.*

He is also likely to further disclose his old culture orientation by adding:

> *Don't worry about a thing. You'll be secure with me. I'll take care of everything.*

What should she do if she receives such a proposal? Many women have faced this situation, and have missed its subtle trap. Too often, they are unaware of the dangers, accept the proposal, and move in just like the princess in the television show. Almost universally, the first thing they do once they are married is to redecorate the interior of the house. While this is a natural desire to both rid the house of evidence of any prior female occupancy as well as assert her own dominion and control, the danger here is that her focus remains on this superficial activity where the issues are really much deeper and more important to her security. There is a tendency to relax and assume all is well once the redecoration is completed. She may also be lulled into a false sense of security because her new spouse understands her need to redecorate, and willingly cooperates with her plans.

The outward expression of possession is not the important issue. New curtains and wall paint do not change title to the castle or assert any form of ownership. If she is not alert, she may find herself the pauper princess trapped in the prince's castle right out of the old culture image. Her willingness to pursue a relationship should be centered on his eagerness to share the ownership of the home where they will live, not his willingness for her to "just move in and don't worry about a thing. Trust me, I'll take care of you." In our example, the young woman was forewarned by the way the male spoke. His words told her he is strictly old culture. He made it clear and in no uncertain terms that the castle is his, and it is going to stay that way. He sees the woman as the pauper princess of the old fable story and not as a true partner. When he says, "Marry me and be my wife," he is thinking in terms of the old culture story. We know this because he uses the old culture language of "my wife" which to most transitional people is a red flag and implies "my wife and personal possession." Transitional males do not use the phrase "my wife" because they are sensitive to the old culture possessory interpretation, just as transitional women also avoid the phrase "my husband." Transitional spouses have names and are respected as individuals with personal standing.

Again, of most importance, the male in our example says:

"All you have to do is move in."

This phrase is a clear warning of his old culture belief that the castle of the image belongs to the knight. In terms of the image, the knight in shining armor is luring the woman to be his pauper princess and move into his castle. He is telling her in no uncertain terms that the castle is his and his alone. Further, he sees her as the princess in the image, subordinate and submissive, over whom he plans to be lord and master and assert dominion and control. Make no mistake; she is entering his domain on his terms. Every woman should be aware of the old culture lure of the castle as a place of refuge. The security she seeks may not be what it appears on the surface. She needs to be wary in such a situation.

Always listen to the language a potential mate uses. At the same time, be wary that looks and first impressions can be deceiving. Most suitors will be on their best behavior until a potential mate has been snared into the marriage ceremony. During courtship, a potential mate may appear to be the most wonderful human being on the face of the earth, but one must be aware that the future conduct of this person is determined by the degree the old culture images control their thoughts and behavior.

Often, the only device to help draw out the old culture orientation is to develop awareness of the signs that give the person away. If a woman is fortunate, the old culture male will expose his social orientation in time to save her a lot of trouble and grief. His answers and responses to direct questions are often the most important warnings she will have of an old culture orientation. However, don't forget that what has been said about males can also be applied to females. A woman who is old culture looking for an old culture husband with a castle, is not focused on individual personalities or characteristics of potential mates, whereas transitional women are looking for true partners. Transitional women are not looking for old culture men who will dominate and control them, and they are wary of being lured into a castle they do not own. Property ownership is just one issue potential spouses need to agree on before they formalize a relationship. Men need to be alert to the feelings of their espoused partner.

The most important danger for the individual personally, is that people with an old culture bias and people with a transitional bias are incompatible, and do not make good marriage partners. If potential partners share the same social orientation, they have the foundation for developing a solid relationship, but if they do not, they should expect difficulties to develop from the very beginning. Just remember, where social orientations do not match, the chances for a successful marriage are low to non-existent. Often more time and money is spent on the ceremony in an attempt to cover a weak relationship. Although there are no studies that tie success in marriage to the amount spent on the ceremony, a strong emotional relationship does not require marriage. Stripped to its most basic element, marriage is a legal relationship about property and property rights. The ownership of the castle is one of the primary issues involved in the marriage relationship. More often than not, the legal issues of marriage are ignored going into the marriage and then become an enormous obstacle on the way out.

From our illustrations of who owns the property, the knowledge that marriage itself does not change ownership is clear. The husband who owned the property in his own name prior to the marriage continues to own the property after the marriage. Be advised, however, that the degree of enforcement over time is subject to the laws in each state and how far they have adopted the concept that husband and wife are one. In most states, the non-owner spouse is given some statutory rights in the family residence, but for accurate information for specific individual rights consultation with a real estate attorney in the state where the property is located is necessary.

The issue of ownership should be of interest to everyone who is about to make a major marital commitment, especially if they have small children. The real issue is what happens if a new spouse moves into a home owned exclusively by the other spouse, and they later divorce. State laws that protect the possessory rights of non-owner spouses often provide little protection on divorce. In addition, such laws seldom protect the non-owner spouse's children if something happens to the biological parent.

Before a female accepts a marriage proposal, she is advised to think through her own personal and financial circumstances and then, with knowledge of the laws of the state where any real property owned is located, make realistic decisions. All too frequently individuals believe that the law in one state that they are familiar with is the same in an adjoining state. This is a mistaken assumption that is compounded by the fact that spousal possessory laws vary significantly from state to state and are often limited to the marital residence. In many states, such rights exist only as long as the castle remains the principal marital residence.

A transitional woman will not accept a marriage proposal unless it involves receiving an acceptable interest in the property where she and her children will live. The question most often asked is how to raise the question about such a sensitive matter. Some people think the issue is not important, and assume it can be raised later after the marriage ceremony, but they are only deluding themselves. It is a core issue to any new marital relationship. In today's world, a person can have an affair anytime and can live with someone without marriage. Some people think that marriage is about emotion, but it is a legal relationship about property and property rights as most people quickly discover on a visit to the warehouse of failed marriages. If a woman has to ask about title to the castle after the ceremony, she is at an extreme disadvantage. The ownership of the castle is the cornerstone of the legal relationship. If she decides to raise the question for the first time once she is married, some of the common responses to her inquiry are likely to be:

> I thought I was a good provider.
> I said I'd take care of everything.
> What have I done wrong?
> You must want a divorce.
> Silence.

Notice that none of these responses answer the question she asked. The last two are the most important because he is saying that he interpreted her silence through the courtship and marriage ceremony as her acquiescence to the knight owning his castle in his own name, which was his unstated but clearly implied condition to entering the marriage relationship. For this reason, he sees her question after the ceremony as a challenge to the marriage relationship. A woman must take into account her own personal and financial circumstances to decide whether she has enough assets to take care of herself if the marriage either does not work out or her husband dies leaving her on her own. She must realize that in the old culture images, no one ever dies, so an old culture husband usually doesn't accept death and is unlikely to look out for her in the event he predeceases her.

The primary concern for every woman with children must be what happens to her children if she dies while they are married. This is an especially important question when she is living in a house she does not own and with a knight who is not the father of her children. One of the most important questions for her is, under what conditions will her children from a prior marriage inherit through her new husband? If she dies, who will care for her children? For example:

> *A man owns his home in his own name. He has two children from his first marriage. The only interest his new wife has under state law is a right to live in the property for life. She also has two children from a previous marriage. Under state law, her children are not his children for inheritance purposes unless he adopts them.*
>
> *She dies with no assets. He never adopts her children. Her children have no interest in the home owned by her surviving husband. When he dies later, his children from his first marriage inherit the house.*

A sample response for the transitional female to the old culture male who proposes marriage and invites her to move into his home might be:

> *I love you, but I can't live with you. I'm a human being, and I need to be treated like one. I'm not your possession. If you do not understand my need to protect my children by putting title to the home in both our names we have no future together.*

Every male who owns a home in his own name needs to be sensitive to this concern. The woman's comment may seem a little harsh, but the message is clear. Some people say that he could provide for her children in a will, but the reality is that if he did not think enough to include her on the deed or adopt her children, it is unlikely he would include them in a will. There's an even greater danger that even if he did include them in a will he can always change his will at any time up until the day of his death.

When it comes to property rights, people tend to focus on their own natural children and other blood relatives to inherit the property, not adopted or step children. We like to think this is a country based on equality, but the family into which we are born determines the circumstances in our lives. This preserves the old traditions of blood relationships from across the sea. In fact, our intestate succession laws were originally based on marriage and blood relations for determining property ownership. These laws continue to be the foundation for our society today. The bond of culture and tradition is strong, but so too is the bond of blood relationships when it comes to property rights no matter how transitional we may believe we are. Everyone must decide the extent to which ownership of the marital home is important before formalizing a relationship where one moves into a home he/she does not own.

Do not rely on a copy or even an original deed to prove a certain set of facts exist regarding property ownership. A deed in and of itself proves absolutely nothing. Only an attorney can conduct a title search and evaluate the evidence of title and authenticity of the deed as evidence of ownership of the castle. For example:

> *To induce a woman to marry him, a man showed the woman a copy of a recorded deed that showed he was the sole owner of a certain property. To demonstrate his good faith, he took her to a notary where he signed a new deed conveying the property over to both of them.*

> *Thinking she was protected, she went ahead with the marriage. Later she found that after the deed he showed her was recorded, he signed a second deed to add his first wife. When they were divorced, the property was awarded to his first wife. The new deed he showed his second wife conveyed nothing because he had nothing to convey. Under the divorce settlement from his first marriage, he had the right to possession for two years. At the end of the two-year period, his first wife had the right to evict them.*

The second wife made the mistake of not seeking legal advice when she was first shown the deed, so no title search was made. She mistakenly relied solely on the deed to bear up the validity of the documents he showed her. This was a serious error.

For a person with children, a second marriage has a different meaning than it does for someone entering into a first relationship. The emotional issues so important in the first marriage at a young age can take second place to economic reality in a second or subsequent marriage. The primary factor is always the degree to which the persons involved are old culture.

The key to every real estate transaction is the need to ask questions. Only by increasing the level of awareness of the real situation can an individual recognize the issues involved. Finding the right questions to ask rather than acting automatically and relying on old traditions, customs, habits, and assumptions can aid the individual in avoiding the potential dangers possible in every real estate transaction. To develop the awareness of the questions to ask, find a real estate attorney who practices in the state where the property is located and schedule some time to discuss your specific circumstances. This action should help avert some of the dangers in any real estate transaction. Just be aware that no attorney owns a crystal ball. If one can't describe their concerns, the attorney cannot read any one's mind. Attorneys also need to know personal goals and personal and financial circumstances to best advise their client on how to accomplish the goals in light of applicable state law.

While the examples in this chapter have focused on transactions where property is transferred to an individual, the next chapter will deal with examples where ownership involves more than one person.

CHAPTER EIGHT: TENANTS IN COMMON

The concept of tenancy in common is much like the concept of individual ownership. In a way, it is simply a number of individual ownerships in the same property. Each tenant in common has an undivided share, like the interest of an individual owner, can be sold or transferred without the permission of the other owners. The interest of a tenant in common can also be mortgaged, and even seized by creditors. In addition, it can be inherited by heirs at law or included in a will.

The difference between the interest of the tenant in common and the individual owner is that the parties share both ownership and possession with the other tenants in common. For example:

> *Anne's mother is the owner in her own name of what was her childhood home. She has a brother. When her mother died, both Anne and her brother inherited the house as tenants in common. Each has an undivided one half interest in the property.*

This example of tenants in common with owners related by blood is the most frequently used form of tenancy in common. The undivided share is an asset that belongs to each party personally. Of course, the tax bill and costs of operation and maintenance for the entire property are billed to one of the parties, so all the co-tenants must arrange for payment of all common expenses. In addition, the parties must negotiate an occupancy agreement since each party has an equal right to use the property. There is no limit to the number of tenants in common that could exist in one property. People marry, die, and divorce. They can sell and mortgage their interests and can lose their undivided share to creditors, so title can become complicated very quickly where multiple owners are involved in the same property.

Tenancy in common is not just used between people who are related by blood or marriage. This estate is also a common way for economic participants to share ownership. When the parties use varying degrees of participation where one party owns an undivided share different from the others, this is usually evidence of an uneven economic participation. For example:

> *James T. Rowe and William Williams are business partners. They buy a parcel of land on which they plan to build a manufacturing plant. James Rowe invests sixty thousand dollars and William puts up forty thousand dollars. They take title as James T. Rowe as to an undivided sixty percent interest and William Williams as to an undivided forty percent interest.*

The use of tenancy in common can be created by grant as in the above example, or it can be created by reservation. For example:

> *Sandy's mother owns the family home in her name only. She gives her daughter, Amy, a deed to an undivided one half interest. Sandy's mother has created an interest in the property for Amy by grant, and at the same time reserved an undivided one half interest for herself, since she originally owned the property in her name only. She did not yet give up the other one half interest. Sandy and her daughter are each tenants in common as to an undivided one half interest.*

If a deed or will simply lists the names of the persons who will receive the property but does not designate the relationship between them, the grant will be construed as giving all the property to the designated persons equally as tenants in common. For example:

> James Rowe deeds the family vacation house to his children as follows:
>
> to Robert Rowe, Sally Smith, and Mary Williams.

Since there is no description of the nature of the estate or the extent each will take, the grant will be of one hundred percent of the property with each receiving an undivided one-third interest as tenants in common.

The dangers in the use of the tenancy in common are very similar to those of individual ownership. These dangers can appear in a deed to the parties or by the actions in transferring property to others, just like the examples of individual property ownership in the last chapter.

Anyone who is likely to receive an interest in a property as a tenant in common may want to discuss the proposed transaction with an attorney before the grantor completes it, for a number of reasons in addition to the ones raised in the last chapter. First, the maintenance of the property may be so expensive, individual parties may not easily handle the undivided share of the costs, forcing the parties to consider liquidating his/her interest as soon as possible. In such case, any one of the parties might want to induce the owner to convey a sum of cash instead of participation in ownership in the property. If all parties are still interested in owning property, each may, instead, buy property on his/her own that fits his/her budget rather than share the expenses of one property.

There are several other reasons being a tenant in common may not be right for the individual. Some of these include the following:

> The bills for taxes, utilities, maintenance, mortgages, repairs cannot be subdivided. This fact requires one co-tenant to assume responsibility for managing the property on behalf of all co-tenants. Such an arrangement may not be acceptable to all the owners.
>
> The co-tenants must all be mature enough to work together to manage the property. If there are any disagreements the property can suffer and the value may drop.
>
> Each co-tenant has the right of occupancy. Allocating a schedule of occupancy can create problems. If one co-tenant lives close to the property and others are far away, occupancy is often not equitable. Distance to the property can also impact on management because those living closest often wind up with an inequitable share of the management obligation.
>
> The fact that each co-tenant may have a different capacity to pay his or her share of the obligations may create friction.
>
> Co-owners can have conflicting interests. When an undivided interest is mortgaged or sold to strangers to generate funds for other purposes, the relationships between the owners will change.

Obviously, the pitfalls in selecting tenancy in common is that it is easy to assume that the right thing to do is to give your children certain property as tenants in common where each will have an equal undivided interest. The danger is that parents often see their children as equal to each other in abilities and interests. In addition, they often do not visualize their children as grown up with families of their own.

Children are unique individual human beings. As they grow up, their differences will become more pronounced. This means that what is right for one child may not be good for another, and their abilities and interests will not be as identical as their parents often assume. One child may be a good property manager, and the other may have a lack in management interest or skills. Another child may want to rent the property, while the other may want to sell it. One may mortgage their interest to generate cash for other purposes, and one may lose their interest to a creditor. On the other hand, economic business participants in property usually share the same objectives and interests so working together may not be a problem if this attitude is shared. All these factors must be assessed before transferring property to individuals as tenants in common. What appears as a simple way to distribute assets can be far more complex than it first appears.

Whether receiving or transferring real estate, the parties need to remember that one of the greatest pitfalls of tenancy in common is that the value or equity assumed to apply to an undivided interest may not be what it appears. Even though the property is appraised to determine its value, another factor has a greater influence on value than an appraisal. For example:

> *Stan owns a vacant lot appraised for $100,000.00 with no mortgage. He has two children so he assumes if he deeds the property to his children as tenants in common, they will each receive equity or value of $50,000.00.*

This example illustrates the common assumption that can trap the unwary. A fractional interest in property is not usually marketable to the general public. In reviewing the real estate section of any newspaper, one will not see listings of fractional interests in residential property. For the same reason, the owner of a fractional interest will find few sources for a mortgage of a fractional interest as security for a loan. All too often the only market for fractional interests is the other tenant(s) in common in the same property.

This fact alone means that to sell a fractional interest to raise cash to pay taxes or maintenance costs, one will probably have to turn to the very limited market consisting solely of the other owners. This often means the party selling his/her interest may not receive the full, appraised value of the fractional interest. If under duress, one has to accept what a willing buyer is willing to pay from this very limited number of potential buyers, the other tenants in common.

Most of the time, an internal sale to other co-tenants will net less than the interest is worth. If used as a conveyance from parents to their children, all too often the value of the divided interests are less than estimated when given to the children as tenants in common. Nevertheless, whatever the details of the situation, the real issue remains that fractional interests often have a limited market value.

The only way to obtain the full value of a fractional interest is to join with all the other fractional interest holders and sell the property in total. This action is then marketable to the public and may be more difficult than it appears. The ability to market the entire property at one time means that all the fractional interest holders must be in agreement not only to sell, but also as to the terms of the sale. For these reasons it is sometimes better for an owner to liquidate property, and distribute cash so each child can go their own way instead of being bound to each other as co-tenants.

To illustrate the point, the following are some of the issues requiring total cooperation of all co-tenants:

> When to sell
> Whether to use a broker and which broker to use
> What terms to offer
> What price to accept
> What improvements should be made before listing
> What repairs should be made before closing
> What costs should be paid at closing

Because no two people are alike, even if related by blood, frequently obtaining cooperation on any of the above issues can sometimes be difficult if not impossible. Relationship by blood does not guarantee the same level of shared interest that is required for successful co-ownership of property, but frequently leads to family schisms and bad feelings.

The reality is that tenants in common are partners. The best partnerships are those created by common interests and goals. Tenancies in common are more likely to be successful when created by shared economic objectives. Failure to take into account the fact that creating a tenancy in common between children whose relationship is by blood alone will often lead to unintended consequences. For example:

> *Mary Smith has two daughters, Lisa and Sue. Both are in their early twenties. Mary assumes they are ready to become owners so she executes a deed to each for an undivided one-third interest in the old family home where Mary continues to live. Mary, Lisa, and Sue each have an undivided one-third interest in the house.*
>
> *Lisa marries but ends up in divorce court. As a part of the settlement agreement, she deeds her undivided one-third interest to her former husband. Sue puts a mortgage on her interest to finance a trip to the Caribbean where she meets and elopes with the love of her life. The mortgage company is forced to foreclose the mortgage, leaving Mary holding an undivided one-third interest with her daughter's former husband and the mortgage company each with an undivided one-third interest.*

Another danger is the decision to convey property to children before all the consequences of such an action have been considered. The first question is whether the owner is deeding the property before being ready to absolutely relinquish title. Conveyances of real estate are final acts. No one can reverse the conveyance once completed. As adults, the parties to the transaction are responsible for the results of their actions. The question is whether there would ever be a need for the property back due to subsequent changes in circumstances. Once an owner is sure he/she is ready to release ownership of the property, the next question is whether the recipients are ready to accept the responsibility of property ownership. The third issue is whether the transfer is set up to use the best type of ownership between the parties.

If conveying property to children, one may think they will inherit from each other so the property will stay in the family. One needs to remember that children will marry and have families of their own, causing the human dynamics between children and parents to change. Marriage, death, divorce, mortgages, and sales are all events that change the dynamics between the owners of undivided interests in a tenancy in common. Think through the issues carefully and do not act automatically when deciding to create a tenancy in common.

Before leaving the concept of tenancy in common, it is important to address the question that no one asks. The question for us is, can people who are married to each other own their home as tenants in common?

The answer is yes, but the fact is they very seldom do. The reason the tenancy in common is almost never used between married people is easily explained by the influence of the first image of the merger of the parties together as one. The tenancy in common creates two separate ownership estates, whereas married people are seen as one. Because the tenancy in common is inconsistent with our internal image of married people as one, other types of ownership are selected automatically without thinking. Other types of ownership have aspects that more closely fit the concept of merger. Thus, the old culture danger is that the tenancy in common is not considered when, in fact, it is a valid option, even for people married to each other. The tenancy in common should be considered between married people especially when one spouse has children from a prior marriage and the children are not adopted by the other spouse. For example:

> *Richard Rowe and Mary Rowe are married to each other. Mary has children from her first marriage. Richard does not adopt her children. They live in a state where her children cannot inherit from Richard unless he adopts them.*

If the castle is owned by Richard and Mary as tenants in common and she dies first, her undivided one half interest becomes an asset in her estate. His undivided one half interest remains owned by him individually. If she dies without a will, Richard will receive some interest in her property as determined under state law. He will be an heir along with her children, and they will receive distributions determined by the applicable state inheritance law. If she dies with a will leaving all her interest in the castle to her children, in most states Richard will have the right to take an elective share in her property, and her children would receive that part of her interest in the castle that remained.

In some states, the costs of administration of the estate, legal fees, debts, and cost of last illness must be paid first from her estate before distribution to heirs, devisees, or elective share. Thus, the fractional interest in the property may have to be sold to pay these costs. In such case, her children would receive no interest in the castle. In some cases the actual distribution between the husband and the children may force a sale of the interest in the castle unless the husband and the children can reach an agreement among themselves. In any case, her children may receive a distribution from her estate, but there is no guarantee they will have an interest in the castle. The distributions to heirs come from the net estate that remains after the payment of costs.

If her estate is solvent and her undivided one half interest in the castle is still in the estate, then there must be a distribution between the husband and the children. Again, the castle may need to be sold to generate funds to make the distributions unless the husband and the children reach an agreement among themselves. As in the above case, her children may receive a distribution from her estate with no guarantee of having an interest in the castle.

If she dies with a will and leaves her interest in the castle to her children, the payment of costs can again force the sale of the undivided one half interest in the castle. In addition, her husband will usually have a statuary right to elect to take an interest in the estate if he is not satisfied with the provision for him in her will. His election can force a sale of the castle to generate funds to make this distribution if her estate has funds to pay his share of the estate. Only then would the interest in the castle be available for distribution to her children.

The advantage of the tenancy in common between married people exists primarily when the woman transfers her undivided interest to her children during her lifetime. In doing so, her undivided interest will not be an asset in her estate eliminating any risk that her interest in the property does not pass ownership to her children. Assuming that the castle represents the most important and valuable financial asset a woman will own in her lifetime, her primary interest is to provide for her children when she dies. The tenancy in common gives her the ability to be sure that her children will have some interest in the castle. This ability to provide for the interests of her children does not exist in the ownership options that are usually selected automatically by married couples.

Remember, if both spouses own the castle and the husband dies first, she will have the same rights as surviving spouse in his property as he has in hers. His undivided one half interest will be an asset in his estate and his spouse will have the right to select a statutory share in his property. In many states, if he has no children, she will inherit all of his estate. The same rule applies for the payment of costs before distribution of the net estate will apply to his estate just like hers. In states where her statutory interest does not have precedence, it is also possible that his undivided one half interest may have to be sold to pay costs. He also has the ability to convey his undivided one half interest to anyone he selects during his lifetime, as long as he does so in his written and properly executed will.

To understand why tenancy in common is so often overlooked as an ownership device, a review of the types of ownership that are selected as alternatives and a knowledge of the potential dangers of each allows one to evaluate the consequences of each type for their particular individual situation.

In each of the situations where a fractional interest must be sold to pay costs to settle an estate, the comments on the market value of fractional interests must be taken into account. In spite of its disadvantages, the tenancy in common may be the right device for owning property even between people who are married to each other. This is especially true where one spouse has children from a prior marriage due to the risks involved in the alternative estates usually selected. Once aware of the advantages, disadvantages and potential dangers of the tenancy in common, one can examine the alternative types of multiple ownership where the element of survivorship changes the relationship between owners in a fundamental way. In these estates there can be a special risk to the spouse who has children from a prior marriage.

CHAPTER NINE: JOINT TENANCY

The vehicle of joint tenancy, in some ways, is very similar to tenancy in common, differing only in some very simple but significant ways. The applicable definition of *joint* in Webster's II New Riverside Dictionary provides a flavor of this type of tenancy:

--- United in identity of interest or liability
--- Sharing with another or others (such as joint owners)
--- Shared by or common to two or more
--- Formed or marked by cooperation

A tenancy in common can be created by grant or reservation at different times and for different periods of time during the lifetime of property ownership. To create a joint tenancy, the conveyance must include all one hundred percent interest in the property at one time and in one instrument. In addition, the conveyance must include equal interests to all recipients. One cannot create a joint tenancy by reservation in part. For example:

> *I give to my three children, Michael, Janet, and Sally, the beach house, as joint tenants with rights of survivorship and not as tenants in common.*

State laws vary, but in general, the above language is the key to creating a joint tenancy in property ownership. Notice that the conveyance must clearly differentiate the joint tenancy from a tenancy in common. In the example, all three named individuals own the property equally and their interest is created at the same time, including the element of survivorship between them. These are the key characteristics of the joint tenancy. The basic concept of the joint tenancy is that all grantees own the property together as one and their interests are not divisible. The most common type of joint tenancy involves married couples, because survivorship closely approximates the concept of married people as one.

The vehicle of joint tenancy can create a trap that many people do not see. The danger only exists in some situations so one must be alert to look for it in light of their own personal circumstances. Survivorship means that when one owner dies, the remaining joint tenants own the property as one. They remain the owners by virtue of the fact they have survived. What this means in our example above is that when Michael dies, the property remains owned by Janet and Sally as joint tenants still with rights of survivorship between them. In a tenancy in common, Michael's undivided fractional interest would have been an asset in his estate and passed to his heirs. In the joint tenancy, his interest expired automatically on his death and there is no longer an asset in his name upon his death and no portion of ownership or rights of ownership pass to his heirs.

Using the above example, if Sally dies next, her interest also expires at her death. Janet then owns the property wholly, in her name individually. If the three children in this example are very young when the conveyance is created, the use of the survivorship element makes sense. If something happens to one minor child, chances are that the child owns no other assets. Then the survivorship avoids the costs and inconveniences of probating the estate of the child that dies. Usually parents want property to be owned by all of their children. The selection of the survivorship estate means the remaining children continue to own the property equally between them with no inconvenience or hassle. The change in ownership on death of the first child takes place automatically with the expiration of the interest of the deceased child.

However, there is a danger once three children in the above example grow up and Michael has a wife and small children when he dies. His wife and children receive no interest in the property because it is owned in joint tenancy with his sisters. When Sally dies several years later, divorced with two small children, Janet becomes the sole owner individually. She is the surviving joint tenant. Sally's children also receive nothing.

Notice that the passage of time has changed everything. While most parents desire the joint tenancy between their children when they are young, they are usually appalled at the inequitable and arbitrary distribution that occurs when the children are grown and have their own families. Most parents would be far more concerned about their grandchildren and the spouses of their children, and would not simply cut them off solely due to the consequence of their death. There are situations where survivorship is the appropriate ownership vehicle to use, and there are times when it creates unanticipated and unacceptable results. When setting up property ownership with survivorship options, one must consider the passage of time in setting up the initial estate since it may not come into play until many years later. Awareness of the consequences of its use is the key to avoiding its pitfalls. Careful planning for the future is crucial to the process of selecting the right estate to meet the desired results considering one's personal situation and goals.

Consider another example where the facts change and the reader is one of the three children who receive property as a joint tenant with rights of survivorship. In this example, all three children are adults, are married and have children of their own. Assume also that the property and land is very valuable. Understanding the dangers of survivorship and the inequities it can create, one may want to change the estate to the more equitable tenancy in common.

What can the parties do? Once the estate is established, the owners cannot go back to the parents because they conveyed all of their interests in the property. They are former owners and no longer have the power to change anything. However, one can approach the other co-tenants in the hope of inducing them to join in changing the conveyance to create a tenancy in common. To accomplish this end, all co-tenants must agree and use an attorney to ensure that the process and documentation are done properly.

The other characteristic that differentiates a joint tenancy from a tenancy in common is that all the owners hold title together equally. That is, you cannot create a joint tenancy with unequal shares. For Example:

> *I give to my grandson, James an undivided sixty percent and to my daughter Samantha an undivided forty percent.*

This example creates a tenancy in common even if the survivorship language of a joint tenancy is added because the owners do not share equally. To create the joint estate, all parties must own the property equally, no matter how many owners there may be. In a joint tenancy, all parties own the property together as one. Like the tenancy in common, they also have the equal right of possession, but they cannot transfer or mortgage their undivided interest and maintain the estate.

The parents of the three children knew, that as minors, their children could not sell or mortgage the property on their own so the property would be protected. If a conveyance or mortgage was necessary when the children were still minors, in most states, a legal guardian would be required to act on their behalf. The guardian would be responsible to the court to protect the interest of the minors. In most states, the conveyance of real estate, no matter how nominal in value, requires a formal court approved guardianship for joint estates rather than allowing parents to simply act as the natural guardians of their children.

When deciding which type of ownership to use when preparing conveyances to relatives, it is extremely difficult to anticipate all the possibilities that could take place. However, one should take into account some very simple facts:

- --- Minor children will grow up and become adults
- --- Adult children will marry and have children of their own
- --- Everyone is an individual and their interests and desires differ
- --- Everyone will die sometime.
- --- Some people are mature at an early age and some never mature
- --- Mental capacity and freedom from undue influence can change

In spite of having used an example with three joint tenants, the survivorship estate is most often used between two people who are married to each other. Although this is true, the joint tenancy estate is available to anyone, and there is no requirement that the parties be related by blood or marriage. Even though joint tenancy is most commonly used by married couples when they buy their primary residence, the fact that survivorship is selected in almost all residential real estate transactions for married couples is due to our old culture fable where marriage is the merger of the two together as one. Notice that the merger of the female back into the male is not a direct part of the survivorship estate. However, it plays an indirect role in that the old culture male does not accept his own death because the knight in the fable lives forever. Usually, he believes that on the death of his wife the castle will be his alone. In the fable image, only knights own castles. The husband, as knight, does not want the alternative tenancy in common because it would require that he recognize his wife as an equal human being, and multiple ownership is inconsistent with the old image. He is also concerned that on her death he might not receive all the interest in the castle because as a co-tenant she can do whatever she wants with her interest, such as convey her interest to her children. The knight never imagines that his princess might outlive him and be the sole owner of the castle. This very real possibility is inconsistent with the fable image.

What usually happens is that the princess yields all decisions about the castle to the knight, acquiescing to whatever he decides. Too often she doesn't have any real, legal knowledge about property and ownership vehicles, so she doesn't know what joint tenancy means. Even if she does, she is likely to be swayed by her own images of old culture thinking. In any case, she often leaves all the decision-making concerning the castle to her knight. As a result, no alternative to the joint tenancy is considered.

The real danger of the joint tenancy estate is even greater than the poor logic behind its selection. The problem is that usually the buyers never get a chance to make the decision whether it is applicable for their personal situation. Our culture has such a powerful hold on us that all too often the closing agents in the transaction simply assume that survivorship is desired between a husband and wife and prepare the paperwork to mirror that concept of the survivorship estate.

This assumption by others is usually ratified and confirmed by the married couple either directly or indirectly by their silence. The buyers don't speak out because they either are not aware they have a choice of ownership estates or they acquiesce to the use of survivorship due to old culture thinking. The real danger is that the buyers are not aware that those preparing the documents will assume they want survivorship and act on their behalf without even asking. The danger is that settlement agents often prepare the closing documents without any real knowledge of the individual circumstances of the buyers and consideration of alternative options is not done.

The key to the joint tenancy estate is that the documents must expressly show the intent to create the estate by using specific language. This language is spelled out precisely in the laws of each state. Beware that sex and marital status have nothing to do with the use of the joint tenancy and do not have an effect on the applicability of the general survivorship estate. The joint tenancy estate is available to everyone. In fact, if the buyers are not married or do not appear to be married to each other, the presumption of others will be that the buyers do not want a joint tenancy estate. The assumption exists only in the situation where the buyers appear to be married to each other and comes out of the old culture bias that married people are one.

The danger lies with the agent preparing the real estate contract. The agent will often indicate the use of the estate between the buyers on the face of the contract where the buyers' names are provided. This assumption is doubly dangerous because the real estate agents involved in the preparation of the contract usually do not mark the full, required language on the contract but merely indicate the selection of the estate in an abbreviated manner such as "IJT" or "jointly."

The latter designation is more dangerous if the deed was actually typed using the word "jointly." Many states would construe the use of jointly to mean tenants in common because the survivorship language was not included. As we have already stated this clause takes more time to fill in, and the person preparing the contract will often use a shorthand abbreviation that is accepted by the parties preparing the closing documents to mean the full phrase is to be used on the deed. The danger is that the buyers, when reviewing the contract before signing it, will not be familiar with the short hand designation and will not be aware that the estate between them has been selected without their knowledge or consent. In some cases, the contract will be prepared with no designation at all and the closing agent makes the assumption survivorship is intended when they prepare the closing documents.

Joint tenancy with right of survivorship may or may not be the right way to own real estate depending on personal circumstances of the buyer(s). Only an analysis of the unique circumstances of the buyers and their desires and objectives can answer the question of whether survivorship is appropriate. Chances are, joint tenancy will simply be applied by custom and habit. Awareness of the danger of culture bias means being alert to the need to know and understand the options available and to speak up and examine the contract preparation process. The danger is that the contract and documents are being prepared automatically, without thinking or considering all options. Continuing to think in terms of the old culture fable and the fact that culture frequently controls how people act causes reliance on the assumption that men and women are one on marriage. Because the presumption is so strong that married people want survivorship between them, one option to consider when the survivorship estate is not desired is to have the contract prepared as follows:

--- as tenants in common, not as joint tenants
--- and without rights of survivorship

Discuss this option with an attorney in the state where the property is located. Be sure to remember eliminating survivorship is going against culture and will be a fight. One must speak up and act to stop its application automatically due to the culture bias. Other persons or agents may lock a transaction into the joint tenancy survivorship estate. Why would married couples object to its use? For young people right out of school in their first marriage with few assets and no children, the joint tenancy may be the right choice. The primary danger is where there is a second or subsequent marriage, separate property, children from a prior marriage, or significant others in the family to be considered.

The first old culture assumption individuals are likely to make is that children from a first marriage are automatically the children of a second spouse. This is often an erroneous assumption. Lack of awareness of the possibility that this assumption may be wrong may blind the parties from seeing the real pitfall of the joint tenancy. In many states only adopted or biological children can inherit from their father or mother. In these states, parents must do more to make a child that is not a biological child legally entitled to inherit from a new, stepparent. In fact, it is recommended that the new parent legally adopt the child(ren), which requires court action. Here is a simple example:

> *A woman with a small child enters into a second marriage where her new husband does not adopt her child, and under the applicable state law her child does not inherit from him.*

She buys a home with her husband as joint tenants with rights of survivorship. When she dies what happens to the child? If he remarries, generally, it is human nature that the second wife will not have a strong interest in the child of his first wife. When the first wife dies, the husband as the survivor will own the property individually. Her child will have no interest in the property. When he subsequently dies, the child of the first wife is still not his heir unlike his surviving second wife. Even if he adopted his first wife's child, his death leaves the child out of the estate if not included in his will. Unlike his surviving wife, the child has no elective share. It is surprising how often people believe a husband will automatically look after the former wife's children. The problem is that the bonding and care that is assumed to be there, many times is not there. The following are some common examples of comments that illustrate this point:

> --- My children aren't his. I don't like him trying to tell me how to raise them.
> --- You may live with my father, but you are not my mother. No matter what you do you will never replace her.
> --- She just wants my father for herself. She blocks us out because we are not her children. She doesn't want anyone to compete for his attention.

> --- We visit them every once in awhile, but it's always awkward. He just isn't my father.
> --- No matter what I do, she will never accept me as her father.

There are many similar examples that people face every day. Change the relative relationship and add the names of loved ones in the family and the examples may apply to anyone. The inheritance issue goes unnoticed unless the parties involved are aware enough to see it and have the courage to deal with it intelligently. Because the condition of marriage is not a prerequisite for a joint tenancy, the parties could be divorced and still own property in a joint tenancy. The only way to avoid this situation is to have the attorneys and all parties deal with it appropriately through the divorce action.

Joint tenancy is not for everyone in every set of circumstances. The survivorship element may be appropriate in light of unique personal circumstances or it may lead to consequences that are extremely adverse to personal desires. The assumption that it must be used because people are married is incorrect and the result of the old culture bias. Any assumption that available options will be discussed in depth before appearing on the contract and other legal documents is also incorrect.

Be aware that children from a first marriage are not also the children of a new spouse simply as a result of marriage. As a result of false assumptions, don't allow any agent to use the joint tenancy. Such automatic action is a carryover from the old culture bias that on marriage husband and wife are one. In addition, do not assume the real estate agents preparing the closing documents are protecting the buyer's or seller's interests.

Remember that survivorship may make life easier in some cases but can create cruel and unintended consequences in others. The next chapter will show how some states have adopted a special joint tenancy which carries with it the cultural bias in a way that is even more dangerous than the joint tenancy.

CHAPTER TEN: SPECIAL SITUATIONS

A number of states recognize not just the standard joint tenancy that we discussed in Chapter Nine, but a special kind of joint tenancy that exists only between husband and wife. This estate is often referred to as an estate by the entireties, but don't let this fancy term be intimidating. The key distinction between this type of ownership and the regular joint tenancy is very simple. The legal relationship of marriage must exist at the time this estate is created and must exist continuously while the property is owned by the couple. Again, the key element is survivorship. This estate is a good example of the legal adoption of the old culture concept of the merger of the male and female together as one through marriage. However, it does not include the part of the old culture story that merges the female back into the male and dissolves her identity into his. Old culture males will often believe that they live forever as in the story of the knight, so they assume they will be the owner of the castle individually on the death of their wives. For knights, castles in the old culture image are owned by knights, never by princesses. However, in reality, both estates are neutral as to gender and either can survive the other.

Certainly, in those instances where survivorship is important between spouses, the estate is advantageous, because on the death of the first spouse the second becomes the owner of the property individually. Another difference between the special survivorship estate and the regular joint tenancy between married couples is that the special joint tenancy includes protection against creditors. A judgment against only one marital partner does not attach to property owned with the special survivorship estate. The lien of a creditor's judgment against both marital partners attaches because it is against the unity of both as one. This type of ownership law is a clear adoption of the old culture concept of the marital couple as one when it protects against debts that are not against both together.

ECOA is the law that protects loan applicants against culture. This special joint tenancy is a legal adoption of culture on the side of government, first to protect married owners against individual judgment holders and second to provide the survivorship element specifically for people who are married. However, this estate is a clear adoption of the old culture bias of married people as one. In those cases where survivorship is not appropriate in light of the unique personal and financial circumstances of the parties, both the special joint tenancy and regular joint tenancy can lead to unintended and undesired consequences. The following example illustrates this simple concept:

> *Mary Martin and Robert Richards are married and own a home as tenants by the entireties. They are both enrolled in college. Robert executes a student loan for a substantial amount of money. Mary runs up a balance of several thousand dollars on a credit card account in her name only. Neither is a guarantor or cosigner for the debts of the other.*

Neither pays their individual obligations, and their creditors obtain judgments against them individually. Since these judgments are liens only against the assets owned individually, they do not attach to the home owned by them together using the special joint tenancy. The special joint tenancy exists only as long as the parties are married to each other. If the ownership changes to a tenancy in common on divorce, the judgments in the above example would attach, such that Robert's undivided one half interest would be subject to the lien of the judgment by the creditor that made the student loan, and Mary's undivided one half interest would be subject to the lien of the judgment creditor that owns her credit card account.

Another important aspect of this special joint tenancy is that the parties must be married *to each other* in fact when the estate is created. If the parties are not married and the deed is recorded stating that they are, they take title only as tenants in common since the condition of marriage did not exist when they took title. If they are married *after* they take title, they will still own the property as tenants in common because the marriage does not change title. Their subsequent marriage does not create the survivorship estate because they already own the property as tenants in common.

Another danger for the unwary is the fact that some of the states that have adopted this type of ownership do not require any special language to create the special tenancy on the deed. These states will assume the special estate is desired unless the deeds clearly state a contrary intent. For example:

> A deed to James Rowe and Mary Rowe, husband and wife, would create an estate by the entireties if they are married to each other on the date the deed is delivered to them.

> A deed to Mary Smith and James Rowe, wife and husband, would create an estate by the entireties if they are married to each other on the date the deed is delivered to them.

> A deed to James Rowe and Mary Rowe with no language of survivorship or marriage on the deed will create an estate by the entireties in such states if they are married to each other on the date the deed is delivered to them.

In the last example, the danger is that the estate with the survivorship element may exist even though there is absolutely no language of intent. For married couples who do not want the survivorship element of the special joint tenancy, they must express their true intentions on the deed. For example, a deed reads:

> --- to Robert Richards and Mary Richards

Without a clear statement of intent, there is a danger that a third party looking at the deed could not tell the nature of the estate in those states that create a presumption in favor of the special joint tenancy if Robert and Mary are married to each other. Some people have suggested that the estate is clarified with one additional step of including the following language to the grant to Robert and Mary:

> --- as tenants in common and not as joint tenants or tenants by the entireties.

The above wording is merely a suggestion. Take the time to seek the advice of a real estate attorney in the state where the property is located for the correct language to use as married parties who do not want a survivorship estate.
 The following example illustrates how the use of the special joint tenancy can lead to unintended consequences:

> *---I, James T. Rowe, give the beach house to my daughter Mary Smith and her husband Ted Smith, as tenants by the entireties.*

When James Rowe dies a few years later, Mary and Ted have divorced. In states that recognize the special tenancy, the grant is effective when the will is probated and the result would be that Mary receives an undivided one half interest and Ted receives an undivided one half interest as tenants in common because they are no longer married on the date the conveyance is effective. Obviously, James never intended this result to come to pass. If his daughter was not married, it is unlikely he would have wanted the man she divorced to have any interest in the property. His failure to change his will after they divorced created the problem.

Divorce attorneys cannot read minds, nor do they have ESP. One of the assumptions they may make is that it is acceptable to the parties if divorce splits the property into a tenancy in common and where each party has an undivided one half interest. The parties need to express their desires to the attorney if such an arrangement will not work. If title to the property is to be handled differently, the parties also need to be aware that the court usually needs actual service of process of the proceedings on the opposing spouse if their interest in property will be affected by the proceedings.

One must also inform the attorney if property located in another state is involved in a divorce action. Remember, real estate laws differ state by state. It is easy to forget that in some states, a divorce action in a different state may not dissolve a regular joint tenancy and the survivorship element may still be in place. Title to all property in both names needs to be addressed in the divorce proceedings. Marriage is a legal relationship concerning property and financial matters, and divorce is a legal proceeding that deals with property and financial matters after the marriage fails. No attorney can properly represent a client without knowledge of the property owned by both parties and any special personal and financial circumstances. The parties are responsible for ensuring that all relevant information is provided to the attorneys so that representation is effective and settles all matters.

Often, the parties believe that the best strategy in a divorce action is to obtain exclusive title to the castle. This often appears to be a good strategy because residential real estate will generally increase in value faster than most other assets owned. However, the one who receives the residence also assumes all obligations including insurance, utilities, mortgage payments, taxes and all other miscellaneous expenses. If the cost to carry the property is so great, the successful party may be forced into an immediate sale if unable to keep up expenses. The eventual sale proceeds depend not on assessed value but the pressure may force the seller to take whatever offer settles the property quickly.

Preferably, the property should be sold when the market for the property is high. Selling when the market is low is not favorable. The optimum situation is when the seller may control when a property is placed on the market, not to sell under pressure. Many divorce decrees have been based on what is assumed to be the appraised value of property. If the property must be sold quickly, the sale may not produce the equity anticipated or what the appraisal shows.

Also be aware that the joint tenancy and the special joint tenancy are usually not restricted to the residence. Both vehicles can be applied to other residential and commercial property. The common danger of a divorce action is that the residence is carefully dealt with but the beach house or commercial property is often overlooked. When this happens, the divorce simply splits the ownership into a tenancy in common creating a quasi partnership with the parties.

The danger in the special joint tenancy is the same as that of the joint tenancy. Closing agents are likely to assume that married couples desire joint tenancy. The real estate documents beginning with the contract are prepared based on this assumption. Once again, one must decide if survivorship is desirable in light of special circumstances. Each individual must take the initiative to offset the assumption of survivorship if it is not appropriate to his/her personal situation.

Be advised of two traps waiting to snare the unwary. First, if the contract is simply prepared just showing the names of the parties, remember that some states have adopted the presumption that the survivorship estate is desired even though there is no expression of such intent on the contract. To be safe, the language suggested to offset the assumption should be considered. The second trap to watch for lies in the following phrases:

    --- as joint tenants with rights of survivorship and not as tenants in common
    --- as husband and wife as tenants by the entireties
    --- as husband and wife

These phrases are often not spelled out carefully on the contract. The person who prepares the contract may use an abbreviation just as in the case of the regular joint tenancy. The parties to the contract must watch for the addition or codes after the names printed or typed on the contract such as:

--- IJT
--- H&W
--- ENT
--- SVR

Any designation after the names on a contract should be explained before signing the contract. The designations are likely to be code designations that the survivorship estate is to be used. Remember, chances are these abbreviations may be added without knowledge or approval of the parties based simply on the assumption that married people are one, and people who are married want survivorship simply because they are married. Thus, the danger of the use of the survivorship estate can come from others whether or not they are acting on behalf of the parties. The bias of culture often lulls the individual into complacency. The only way to avoid the power of culture is by being aware of its influence on the real estate transaction. Take the initiative and ask questions. Do not let vestiges of old culture thinking and biases creep into the decision making process or let it take over financial transactions. Old culture thinking can catch anyone when least expected. Being aware of the dangers is the one tool that will help decrease the chances of being caught in an old culture trap. Thus it is important to ask questions before signing anything.

There is nothing wrong with the special survivorship estate. It just may not be the right device for everyone in every situation. The primary example of an inappropriate use of this estate is where children from a first marriage are brought into a second marriage. If the new spouse shows no interest in making the children legitimate heirs, there is a potential for a serious problem. If the biological parent dies first with the survivorship element in the deed to the home, the property passes automatically to the surviving spouse, individually. This leaves biological children with no interest in the castle. For this reason, survivorship is not always the best way to own property between people who are married to each other. The vehicle of tenancy in common offers an alternative that may apply in some circumstances.

Be alert to the fact that in the old culture fable, marriage makes the partners one. This assumption of merger can easily lead to traps for the unwary. The biggest danger to face is that the old culture biases are buried deep in the subconscious. Old culture thinking has influenced property laws in some states more than others. The only way to counter old culture thinking is to develop the awareness of the pitfalls and dangers inherent in every transaction if it is not thoroughly reviewed before committing to it. The greatest danger lies in doing things automatically, without thought and without question. To make this point on how assumptions can trap the unwary, carefully review the following example:

> Ralph Richards and Roxanne Richards are married to each other. They have been looking for a new house for three weeks. At long last, she sees one she likes, but they agree to keep looking for one more week. Ralph decides to surprise her. He meets with the real estate agent and has her prepare a written contract. Because he wants to surprise Roxanne, he has the contract drafted in his name only. He uses his separate checking account to write a check for the down payment so Roxanne will not know what he is doing.
>
> Ralph then goes to his friendly mortgage lender and applies, in his own name, for a purchase money mortgage. Again he applies for the loan in his own name as applicant because he wants to preserve the element of surprise.
>
> Roxanne is a necessary party and must attend the closing because in the state where the property and land is located the spouse of the owner is given a statutory right to live in the marital home. As a result, legally she must sign the mortgage to give the lender a first lien on the property.
>
> Years later, she checks the deed only to be shocked when she does not see her name on the deed. Ralph always talked in terms of them both owning the property.
>
> When Roxanne confronts Ralph, he too is shocked. He feels sure that the closing agent was aware they were married. He assumed that since he told the closing agent about his wife, the documents would be prepared in both names.

This story ends well because Ralph immediately met with his attorney and had a new deed prepared to put both names on the title to the property.

Notice that this situation is the reverse of the usual assumption made by the real estate agents who assume most people want survivorship because they are married. In this case, the buyer assumed that since he was married, everyone knew to prepare the documents in favor of both spouses. He assumed that the contract in one name only would spring into a deed in both names because they are married. Notice that this situation could have had quite a different outcome if Ralph had suffered a severe stroke and was unable to respond in his own behalf before she discovered the status of title.

Real estate is an area of precision. There is no room for assumptions or ambiguity, and there are consequences to all completed actions. Each state has different rules so the consequences of what is done will vary from state to state. For those who may not understand why married couples would not want to use an estate with survivorship through the joint tenancy or through the special joint tenancy, we have three examples to demonstrate where survivorship is not always appropriate:

> *(1) Larry is in his mid fifties. He is raising his sister's son, Steve, who is eighteen. Steve was born with limitations and has the mental capacity of a ten year old child. Several years ago, Larry's sister and her husband, who had been Larry's best friend, died as the result of injuries sustained in an automobile accident.*
>
> *Larry took Steve under his wing and brought him up. In spite of Steve's limitations, Larry has always thought of Steve as his son. To Larry, taking care of Steve was his way of keeping the memory of his sister and his best friend alive. Larry now plans to marry a woman almost fifteen years his junior. The marriage is scheduled to take place in a couple of months so Larry decided to see an attorney before they buy their new home together. The attorney asks Larry how he plans to take care of Steve.*

If Larry and his fiancé had already signed a contract, it might have been drafted to automatically include the language customarily used to identify the survivorship estate. If they bought the property together with the special joint tenancy estate adding their difference in ages to the knowledge that females generally outlive males, it is likely that Larry's new wife would outlive him. The issue then would be what would happen to Steve after Larry was gone. Would the widow have the same motivation to take care of Steve as Larry did? Taking care of an adult with severe limitations would be very difficult, particularly for a new, young wife. Realistically she might find a new romantic interest after Larry is gone. The real issue is, what would happen to the human dynamics even if she did feel some attachment to Steve? The survivorship estate could be the wrong way to own the property in light of Larry's overall financial situation. This simple example illustrates how the decision to use the survivorship estate needs to be thought through very carefully considering personal circumstances in the present and future. For Larry, his personal circumstances were quite different from those of the woman he was about to marry. This is one of the primary situations where survivorship might not apply.

Another situation where a survivorship estate might not work exists where the financial backgrounds of the parties are not equal at the time the estate is created. For example:

> *(2) Arturo Suarez and Adriana Suarez, parents of a young woman who had purchased a townhouse two years earlier, went to an attorney seeking assistance. Their daughter and her new husband did not have the money to buy the townhouse they wanted. The down payment and the funds to close all came from Arturo and Adriana. The twenty thousand dollars they provided represented a substantial part of their savings and retirement. They explained that in exchange for the money they anticipated that on retirement they would be able to move into the first floor bedroom of the townhouse.*

What no one anticipated was the sudden death of their daughter from a blood clot on the brain a year after the marriage and the purchase of the townhouse. She was only twenty-three years old when she died, and her death was totally unexpected. The parents who had lost their daughter so young and in whom they had invested so much of their savings, had no interest in the ownership of the property. The young couple had purchased the property with rights of survivorship. Title was now in the name of their daughter's husband individually as the survivor.

The daughter's former husband had now remarried and he and his new wife had an infant son. The new family was living in the property that had been bought with the funds provided by Arturo and Adriana Suarez, who now faced a difficult if not impossible battle to try to recover any part of their funds. Their interests had not been structured into the transaction and their investment had not been protected. While a fractional interest, life estate, or a mortgage on the property were possible devices that could have been considered, their intent that they should have some interest in the property in exchange for the funds they put up, had not been expressed in writing, so their desires were not taken into account.

Neither the buyers nor Arturo and Adriana obtained legal assistance before the closing so no one knew of the condition to the money other than their deceased daughter. Their desire to be able to live in the property was nothing more than an informal verbal agreement with their daughter, and was now totally unenforceable legally.

Even if counsel had been retained, it is still doubtful that the attorney would have known the desires of Arturo and Adriana unless they carefully described their requirements directly. The old culture orientation of the husband and the old culture bias of all the parties in the transaction that a survivorship estate was the only way for a married couple to take title would most likely have kept anyone from saying anything to the attorney. The real estate agent who prepared the original contract probably assumed that survivorship was appropriate, and, in all likelihood, the young couple didn't realize there was an alternative. The old culture bias of marriage prevailed, and no one looked at the unequal relationship between the buyers or the interests of Arturo and Adriana.

The question for everyone contemplating a real estate purchase is to ask if the structure of the transaction takes into account the special personal and financial needs and circumstances of all parties involved. Hopefully this example increases the level of awareness required so all the important questions will be asked before making any personal commitments in a real estate transaction.

Another situation that brings into question the appropriateness of the use of the special survivorship estate between married persons is the element of time and how it becomes a factor as personal circumstances change. One of the elements that creates a trap is the old culture assumption that everyone lives forever. In the old culture fable, no one ever dies or ages, and things remain as they have always been once the knight brings his princess home to the castle. For example:

> *(3) In the divorce proceedings, James Johnson's first wife was given custody of their daughter. When he met Mary, his present wife, she had two sons, who were both in boarding school out of state. Neither James nor Mary adopted each other's children.*
>
> *During their marriage, they bought three commercial properties. Each one was purchased using a survivorship estate. The children on both sides remained cool to the marriage of James and Mary. The children grew up with little contact with their stepparents and stepsiblings. James and Mary were successful business people and they put their earnings into the properties they owned together and the properties substantially increased in value.*
>
> *Their children did not do as well. Both James' sons married and have small children. Both are struggling to get by on moderate*

level incomes. Jane's daughter is in a drug rehab program, and is not regularly employed, although she now has two children.

James and Mary were involved in a serious auto accident and are both placed in intensive care in the same hospital. Neither is expected to live.

The use of the survivorship estate has created a macabre situation with their children sitting on opposite sides of the visitor's room in the hospital waiting for the first parent to die. Since the three valuable properties are owned with the survivorship estate, the children of the first to die receive nothing while those of the second receive all the property. The jointly held property, now appraised at several million dollars, has created a harsh and probably unintended situation due to the automatic use of the survivorship estate. The old culture fable of husband and wife as one, with survivorship the only option for property ownership was allowed to control the selection of the survivorship estate. James and Mary did not consider the future consequences of its selection on their children if something should happen to them. They did not anticipate the day when they would be gone. They did not take into account that they would not live forever or that their children would grow up and have families of their own.

Whenever survivorship is used, the parties need to be aware the original circumstances that exist when the estate is created will change over time. As a result, the survivorship estate may produce unintended consequences years later. For this reason it is important also to review documentation and finances on a regular basis to adjust for these changes.

There is another dangerous situation that works something like a joint tenancy of which everyone should be aware. The concept merging married people together as one comes into play in our tax laws. The government adopts the merger concept and creates economic incentives for married persons to file joint tax returns. The hidden danger of which many are not aware is that the economic benefit of lower tax rates for joint filings is often offset by the increased risk to the individual participants. Joint filings may sound advantageous, but in both federal and in most states, joint filings incur joint and several responsibility for the data on the returns as well as liability for all taxes due. This means that both parties are individually responsible for all of the taxes due based on the joint data provided.

While filings where the knight is the only one working makes sense in most situations, the two-income family creates a dangerous situation. Married people are not one. They are separate individual human beings. What federal and state government agencies overlook is that a tax return can only be filled against one person's social security number. As a result, one of the marriage partners will have more input and control over the filing of a return than the other. Individuals who divorce after they have filed joint returns during their marriage may painfully discover this.

Government agencies do not care about real world facts or problems. If both spouses sign a return as a joint return and the governments cannot collect the full amount from one spouse, then they will look to the other to collect the money due. If the parties are later divorced and the one against whom government seeks to collect does not have the records, it is of no concern to the government agency. The government agencies see married people who file jointly as one and each is totally liable for all the obligations under any joint return. This increased risk can overshadow any savings accrued by filing jointly.

Many married people feel they have to file jointly because they are married, a dangerous assumption right out of the old culture biases. Thankfully, most government agencies allow individual filings by married people. Each individual person must determine how to file and pay income taxes. Just remember there are options. Do not allow old culture thinking or biases to cause one to act automatically without thinking or exploring options available.

There are also a number of states that have statutes in place called community property laws. Under these statutes, the state gives special recognition of common interests that arise by virtue of the relationship of marriage in determining title to real estate. Property that is acquired during marriage (other than property acquired by inheritance or an individual gift to one spouse) is owned in common by husband and wife with each spouse owning an undivided one-half interest in the property. A number of states have community property statutes, including Arizona. California, Idaho, Louisiana, Nevada, New Mexico, Texas, and Washington. While we have not focused on these statutes, remember the old culture concept that married people are one for certain purposes influences these laws. The laws of these states are different from most other states, so before purchasing property in these states, married persons need to carefully review these statutes.

The examples used in this chapter illustrate the danger of the old culture thinking that married people are one. Such vehicles as survivorship estates, spousal rights, community property laws, and joint tax returns can trap the unwary depending on individual circumstances. Of utmost importance, be alert for the automatic reliance on familiar generalizations and old assumptions that evolve out of old culture thinking. Only by asking questions before acting can the individual avoid old culture traps.

CHAPTER ELEVEN: DANGEROUS ASSUMPTIONS

    As we know, marriage is not magic. When young people with few assets and no children decide to buy a home and apply for financing together, they will have to decide whether to use the tenancy in common or the regular joint tenancy. Even when living in a state that recognizes the special joint tenancy, it only applies if married at the time of taking title. Thus this option may not be an available option, particularly for non-married couples.

    Couples must know what marriage means to each other before purchasing property together. If married after the property is purchased, there is another decision to be made. If the castle is purchased using the tenancy in common after marriage, the element of survivorship may be important. To change the vehicle of ownership on the deed, an attorney is necessary to process the change in title. If regular joint tenancy was used in a state of residency that recognizes the special joint tenancy, legal proceedings are needed to change the estate that exists between the parties. In both situations, marriage does not change title no matter how special the marriage may seem.

    Awareness that the survivorship element of the joint tenancy is not always appropriate can underscore the importance of knowing what are the potential dangerous elements of the survivorship estate. Particular dangers are paramount when the estate is applied automatically in a transaction because the buyers believe it is the only option available to them. The second inherent danger lies with the real estate agents involved in the closing process who often assume the buyers desire survivorship and place the survivorship element in the transaction without the consent or knowledge of the buyers. The old culture image that married people are merged together as one lies buried deeply in each one of us. As a result, we often act automatically without realizing that the culture bias is influencing what we do. This cultural bias can affect the decisions made as potential real estate buyers as well as the real estate agents and attorneys involved in the closing process.

The survivorship element closely approximates the old culture image of married partners merged together as one. Both the regular and special joint tenancy vehicles use the concept that the owners are one such that when one dies the other still owns all of the property. Thus, the old culture bias within pushes us to accept the survivorship estate for married couples, often adopted automatically without thinking, even in situations where it does not apply. The survivorship estates are gender neutral and do not carry the merger of the female back into the male. Either spouse can survive the other. These estates use only the concept of the merger of the male and female together as one. However, do not discount the fact that generally, old culture knights forget that they will not live forever. Knights instinctively believe they will, in the end, own the castle in their own names, contrary to statistics for life expectancy of males versus females. This belief in the old culture concept of the invincibility of the knight lures many old culture males to use the survivorship estate. In a later chapter we will explore this faith in their survivability as misplaced. Remember, the survivorship estate is usually applied automatically in real estate transactions unless the buyers indicate they want to take alternative action.

Since the survivorship estate is assumed to be appropriate for all married couples, the burden falls on the buyer to overcome the bias and properly review the specific situation and documentation before the transaction is completed. Unfortunately, the only way to prevent assumptions from controlling one's life is to take personal responsibility to ensure that the consequences of the transaction match personal goals and desires. As a buyer, one must review the contract and closing documents carefully. Usually the parties in the transaction do not have enough time or contact with the other persons and agents involved in the closing process to be able to anticipate whether the agents are acting automatically and applying the survivorship estate without consent. Asking questions and providing information to the persons and agents handling the transaction in advance of the closing date will assure that the documents reflect the desires of the parties.

In all the examples provided here, note that ECOA does not apply to property ownership. ECOA applies only to creditors when dealing with applicants for credit. However, remember ECOA does state that a female could use her maiden name, a married name, or a combination name. This is true for property ownership as well. Most state laws do not restrict the use of names on real estate documents. The order of names on a document by gender is not covered by ECOA, nor does state law restrict it. Thus, the following options for name designations on contracts and deeds are also available in most states:

> Mary Jane Rowe and James T. Rowe
> Mary Jane Rowe and James T. Rowe, wife and husband
> Mary Jane Smith and James T. Rowe, married to each other
> Mary Jane Smith and James T. Rowe, as joint tenants with rights of survivorship and not as tenants in common

There is a second dangerous assumption that is often made by others. This assumption is that men and women seen together are married to each other. The following example shows how both the assumption of marriage and the survivorship estate can be tied together:

> *The top of page one of the contracts showed the buyers as James T. Rowe and Mary Rowe, but did not show marital status. The buyers signed the last page of the contract but their names were not printed or typed on that page, and their signatures were not clear.*
>
> *The creditor's loan closing instructions showed both names, James T. Rowe and Mary Rowe, H & W, the abbreviation for husband and wife. At the closing, the parties brought a young man about thirteen years of age with them who was introduced as James Rowe, Jr.*
>
> *When presented with the closing documents, Mary refused to sign. She claimed she was not married to James Rowe, and her last name was not Rowe. She explained that her name was Mary Smith, and that was the way she signed the contract and the loan application. The contract was given to her to sign opened to the signature page so she did not see how her name was shown on the first page. She paid no attention to the loan application, but signed her real name on the blank signature line.*
>
> *She explained that she understood the problem because ever since she moved in with James Rowe several years ago, she started receiving mail addressed to Mrs. James Rowe as well as Mary Rowe, but she had not married him because he was already*

> married and had never divorced his wife. The young man who attended the closing was his son from his marriage. Mary had simply moved in with James, and they had lived together and ignored his wife, who had abandoned the family eight years ago.

In the state where the property was located, a non-owner spouse has an interest in the family home. Although unseen for eight years, James Rowe's spouse had a statutory interest in the property and was a necessary party to the mortgage, so the closing had to be cancelled. The creditor was upset with the time wasted and wanted to charge the couple for costs. The lender even considered suing the buyers for fraud. However the lender dropped the matter because the contract did not show marital status and had been prepared by service providers who had also assumed Mary's last name was Rowe. No one was able to clearly read her signature. Mary signed her real name on all the documents and others saw what they wanted to see. No one asked any questions even though her signature was not legible. The other persons involved in the closing had perpetuated the assumption that her last name was Rowe, and that she was married to James.

If the buyers had proceeded to close the way the document were prepared, at best they would have been tenants in common because they were not married. In such case, James Rowe's spouse would still have an interest in the property no matter how the documents were prepared due to the laws where the property was located.

As the example illustrates, no one is immune from making the assumptions that first, a couple is married to each other, and second that they desire the survivorship estate. For these reasons, be aware that real estate agents may make assumptions that are based on observation, not fact. Only by questioning and determining facts will individuals stop the process of adding the survivorship element to the transaction. This example illustrates how people assume men and women are married simply because they are seen together. The old culture need to make poor Adam whole again can affect the ability to perceive reality. This bias can be so strong that without thought, a casual observer may assume that a couple is married to each other in the wrong circumstances.

There is another estate to consider which is generally overlooked in circumstances where it may be valuable. This vehicle is the life estate. One of the reasons the life estate is seldom used is that it is inconsistent with the old culture concept that married people are one and thereby should own their home together as one. To add the interests of other people outside the marriage through the use of the life estate is inconsistent with the simple old culture image of the family consisting of knight and his princess as

Adam's Eve

the exclusive owners of the castle. As a result, the life estate is the most underutilized device to help structure property ownership in a way that best suits personal and financial needs.

If the interference of the old culture bias with the exclusive ownership of the castle by the knight and his princess were eliminated, the life estate would most likely be used more frequently today. The reason this vehicle could help serve families today is that never before in our history have so many households consisted of more than the conventional nuclear family. Households now are not limited to husband, wife and their biological children. For this reason the life estate has a greater practical applicability then ever before. Careful evaluation of family circumstances could show that the life estate as an important valuable vehicle to be used today. A life estate is an estate of possession or occupancy and not one of equitable ownership. An example follows:

> *If Robert Rowe executed and recorded a deed to his daughter, Dorothy, and reserved a life estate for himself, the fact the property substantially increased in value after he deeded the property to her does not have any impact on him. He simply reserved the right to live in the property for the remainder of his life. The true owner or remainder man, Dorothy, is the beneficiary of the increase in value.*

A life estate is the right of the possessor of this estate to occupy the property as long as the holder of the right is alive. The life estate terminates automatically on the death of the holder of the life estate. The key characteristic of the life estate is that there is no property interest left to include as an asset when the holder of the life estate dies. The fact that the life estate terminates on the death of the life tenant is the reason the life estate is a useful device in many circumstances. If the owner of the equity or value in the property decides to sell the property while the life estate exists, the property is not marketable without the joinder of the life estate holder.

A life estate acts as a protection for those who have possessory interests in the property. Neither buyers nor mortgage lenders will deal with property that is subject to the right of a third party to live on or in the property for life unless the holder of the life estate joins in the transaction. Beware that the life tenant is likely to refuse to sign any document that would take away or encumber their interest unless they are assured that some equivalent interest is provided in exchange that gives them the same security as the life estate they are asked to give up or encumber. The most common use of the life estate occurs where an elderly parent transfers property to their children. For example:

> *Mary Richards decides to transfer her home to her daughter and her daughter's new husband. She creates a survivorship estate between them. In addition, to protect her own right to live in the home for as long as she lives, she reserves a life estate. She is not worried about her daughter's motivations and intentions, but she is concerned about what would happen if her daughter predeceased her and her daughter's husband might decide to remarry. The human dynamics in that situation would be unpredictable.*

There is another issue that Mary needs to consider:

> *If her daughter and her daughter's husband divorced, the property might be owned by both or awarded by the court to one or the other. As holder of a life estate in the property, the divorce action would have no jurisdiction over Mary's rights. A life estate would protect her against a loss of residential possession in any of the situations that might arise.*

In the examples used in this chapter to illustrate individual ownership, parents may reserve a life estate for themselves in the deeds they gave as wedding gifts. It may be valuable to review the examples in this chapter with the inclusion of a life estate by the parents to gain perspective on the value of this estate. In the revised examples, the issues as to the life estate would result in maintaining residential possessory rights for the parent.

Before making any changes in favor of a life estate, be aware of a cautionary note for life estates in grants you receive. The truth is that there is not likely to be one. As valuable as the life estate is, this vehicle is not used very often. The life estate could also be created by direct grant from a child giving the estate to a parent. The elderly parent and adult child situations are not the exclusive situations where a life estate could be used, but they are the most common. Remember the example in a prior chapter where Larry was raising his sister's son, Steve who had limited mental capacity. In that example, Larry was considering marriage to a younger woman. The use of a life estate to protect Steve is a possible solution for Larry to protect Steve should something happen to him, leaving Steve alone. However, it was probably not the best alternative since Steve would need financial assistance in addition to a place to stay in the event that Larry predeceased him. A full interest in the property was likely to be more valuable for Steve depending again on Larry's personal and financial circumstances and his ability to provide other assistance for Steve. If Steve were not mentally disabled, the life estate would have been a valid option to protect his right to live in the property.

Of course, the relationship with Larry's new spouse is also a factor that needs to be considered as well. There are no easy answers for Larry because the laws of the specific state where the property is located need to be balanced against the unique needs of the parties in structuring the ownership that is best suited under the circumstances.

There are some dangers in using the life estate. For example:

> *Sally Smith's father reserves a life estate in the deed where he gives property to Sally. When he becomes elderly, infirm, and mentally no longer able to care for himself, he is placed in a nursing home. Sally now wants to sell the house, but her father no longer has the mental capacity to understand the transaction or to sign the deed on his own. A legal guardian is then needed to convey his life estate interest in the property, and the value of the life estate interest will have to be determined by the court.*

The use of a life estate is not appropriate for all circumstances, but it is often an option that should be considered. One of the dangers or pitfalls of the old culture story is that it runs forever. In the fable, everyone lives happily ever after and no one ever dies. The tendency of old culture people is to deny and ignore their own mortality and not to prepare for it. However, even if we accept our mortality, we often fail to consider the fact that it is possible for a child to predecease a parent or grandparent. Over 40,000 people die in this country each year just from automobile accidents alone. There is no monopoly in such cases by any particular group identified by age, sex, marital status or any other designation. All of us have a tendency to assume we will live forever. The key to the success of property and estate transfer is to plan as best we can for the events we can anticipate as possibilities. One of the problems that must be dealt with is the fact that many often do not live long enough to see the consequences of the actions taken, and the results of these actions can be different from what was originally intended.

Being aware of the issues in time to adjust the results based on knowledge and careful analysis is the only solution for a successful planning. The life estate is one tool to consider when making such an analysis, especially for the adult child seeking to protect a parent, even in the event of the unanticipated death of the child. The life estate is not the right device to use in every situation, but for some cases it is well worth considering. Only through a careful analysis of state law and specific needs and goals can the answer of the appropriate solution for each person be determined. For this reason, it is important to review all issues with an attorney who knows the laws of the state where the individuals reside.

When reviewing all the estates discussed in the preceding chapters, in each example the solution to the problems do not require a million person march on Washington D.C. to redress some common problem. The issues raised are all issues resolved at the state level. Individual separate marches on the states need not be considered either. The tools needed to solve the issues already exist within the mechanisms available in each state. Rather, the answer is to become as informed on the issues and options available to identify the problems as they arise and find the most appropriate solution available today.

In this and the preceding chapters, there are many examples where one or more of the persons involved is over the age of fifty-five. When such a person is involved in the situation, it is important to seek the guidance of an attorney who deals with the rights of senior citizens and specializes in what is commonly called "elder law." There are a number of issues unique to this age group that need to be taken into account in any real estate transaction. However, whatever the personal circumstances are, remember the only goal is to increase knowledge and awareness to avoid an automatic reliance on old habits, presumptions, and customs which may not provide the desired results for the unique personal and financial circumstances. Whatever the circumstances, responsibility for one's own life resides within one's self. The best option to avoid the pitfalls that can lead to the automatic reliance on old habits, presumptions and customs is not to allow others make the decisions. Only a careful analysis of state law in light of specific needs can answer the questions of what course of action is appropriate to protect both people and property.

CHAPTER TWELVE: PARTIES TO THE TRANSACTION

From the previous chapters, exposure to the different ownership options available aids in deciding how to own property. The next step on the journey to increased awareness is to understand how real estate transactions are structured. A little knowledge will help to avoid many of the pitfalls that exist from a reliance on old customs and practices that are often undertaken without thought and easily trap the unwary into undesirable results.

The basic foundation of any real estate transaction is a written contract. As per statutes, agreements concerning real estate are not enforceable unless they are in writing. There are many issues involved in the purchase and sale of real estate. A well-written contract addresses each issue in detail. Since the real estate closing is structured from the contract, carefully check the contract for old culture biases that are placed in the document automatically without awareness of the parties. Many contracts are standard forms which providers use for all of their transactions. Thus it is important to read them carefully and add or delete any other issues specific to the property or transaction.

First of all, the names of the parties who will be the new owners and the relationship between them is determined by the way they are described in writing on the contract. One of the first rules of real estate is that the parties on the deed must be prepared exactly as they are shown on the contract. After the contract has been executed, it may be too late to change the way the title will be written, so take the time to precisely set out the full names of the buyers and the way they will hold title.

A second rule to remember is that no one is a party to the transaction unless they have signed the contract. To be listed as a buyer, one must sign the contract to be entitled to the obligation of the seller to convey title to the buyer(s). A signature binds the signer to its obligations, entitlements and benefits so be very sure to know what these items are before agreeing to be a party to the contract.

A third rule is that all changes the buyers or the relationship between them after the contract is signed must be done in writing. The document used to make changes in the parties is called an assignment. Other changes usually take the form of an amendment, but the same rules apply. All contracts can be split into two categories, those that can be freely assigned, and those that contain no right for the buyers to assign their interests to another person. If the contract is assignable and changes in the relationship of the parties are needed, these changes must be in writing in an instrument signed by all the current buyers shown on the contract assigning their interest to all the new parties that will replace them. If the contract contains no right to assign and changes in the parties are desired, all changes must also obtain the written consent of all the sellers preferably on the instrument of assignment to avoid a breach of the contract. Remember, if there is no right to assign, the sellers have no obligation to consent to approval of an assignment. The following are a few examples where a written document is needed to show the changes in names and the relationship between the new buyers:

> I want my husband added on the deed even though he was not a party to the contract.
>
> My wife is on the contract, but I want her left off the deed.
>
> I signed the contract as an individual, but we will be married just before the closing. I assumed my spouse would automatically be added on the deed.
>
> I thought if we were married the day before closing, we would automatically have survivorship between us as of the day of the marriage.
>
> We were married after the contract was signed, but I want to use my married name. I also want to be sure we have a survivorship estate.

Is the old culture bias obvious in each of the above statements? Whenever there is a change in the parties, a written assignment is required from all the original buyers to all the new buyers with the relationship between the new buyers clearly set out. The grantees on the deed will be all those persons listed on the contract as amended or the assignees on the assignment, and no one else. Remember that anyone, married or unmarried, can buy property individually in their own name or with others as tenants in common or as joint tenants. Marital status of its own accord has no affect on determining the buyers, but buyer selection often depends on what marriage means to the parties involved.

Financing is usually related to ownership. If an individual signs the note and is obligated to repay the mortgage debt, they are likely to insist that they be included as an owner. The exception often exists where a parent co-signs or guarantees the note for an adult child and the consideration for their willingness to do so is love and affection. Be aware there may be an assumption by others when an individual buyer is married that the contract should include their spouse, and the contract may be drafted showing both names. However, this assumption is easily discovered when examining the contract before signing it. The more dangerous assumption exists when both spouses are the agreed buyers, and the survivorship element is added automatically and this is not the desire of the parties

Real estate agents should provide the buyers with a checklist showing the options available for owning real estate and let the buyers select the estate they want. If the buyers have questions concerning the alternatives on the form, they can seek legal assistance before signing the contract.

The danger is that the buyers themselves can be influenced by the old culture bias to the extent that they believe married people should buy property together and then proceed to sign the contract as prepared, or select the survivorship estate from the alternatives presented, in either case acting automatically without thinking. For married parties, they must first decide what marriage means to each individual before deciding to buy real estate. Knowing the answers to these issues will help to avoid problems later.

Always remember that the old culture bias is alive and well and deeply imbedded in our thoughts and customs. Only by being aware of its presence can one avoid its dangers. For example, if a man and woman go into a restaurant together and the woman wants to pay the bill, she must make her intentions known to the waiter as soon as possible. The old culture bias is so strongly imbedded in our collective psyches that the waiter or waitress will automatically deliver the bill to the male if not instructed differently. In such case, the old culture male will quickly pay the bill, insensitive to the desire or intent of the woman. Back in the American Dark Ages, old culture males always paid restaurant bills, so the old culture male will act automatically, oblivious to the woman's desires or intentions.

Similarly, to avoid the assumption of the applicability of the survivorship element, a woman must act affirmatively to offset the old culture assumptions. She must let the waiter know the bill is to be brought to her when she places her order. Under the old culture rules of etiquette, the female's order is taken first, so she will usually have time to act before the male is approached. When the meal is complete, a woman who intends to pay the bill must be sure her credit card is in plain view. Even when the credit slip and card are returned for her signature, they are often presented to her male companion. At least in this situation, he will hand the slip over to her since there is nothing he can do with it.

The old culture bias is not only a factor when a woman goes to the restaurant but also when she deals with property owned in her name, individually. A female should never bring a male companion, whether husband, father, brother, or friend with her when she is negotiating for maintenance, repairs, a lease agreement, a mortgage, or a potential sales agreement. The old culture bias remains deep within the people with whom she must negotiate, whether male or female, who will almost always ignore her and address her male companion no matter how many times she tells them she is the owner. The old culture bias causes people see a residence as the castle in the fable. In the fable, the knight is always the owner and in charge of the castle. As a result, the people she meets will reaffirm the old image and address the knight as the owner and not her. Just remember, in the American Dark Ages, princesses did not own castles.

As mentioned previously, the rule concerning buyers on a contract is that all the buyers shown on the contract must sign it or they are not bound by its terms and are not a party to the transaction. For example:

> *James Rowe negotiates to buy a commercial lot. His plans are to build a convenience store on the corner location. Because he believes married people are one, he has the contract prepared to include his wife as a buyer.*
>
> *His wife, realizing that a corner commercial lot might have been a gasoline station site where the owner would be responsible for the extensive environmental clean up costs, refuses to sign the contract.*
>
> *The transaction is closed without her and she is not shown as a party on the deed. She has no obligation for the cleanup costs.*

Then, again, if the business is a success, she may not be a recipient of the proceeds unless governed by marital agreements outside the real estate benefits.

Commonly, there is always a strong old culture pressure for a married woman who desires to buy real estate in her own name to include her husband on the deed. One way to offset this old culture pressure is to simply provide the name she wishes to use as buyer but refuse to provide her marital status because it is not necessary on the contract. Marital status will be an issue when she plans to mortgage or sell the property in a state where the spouse of the individual owner is given a statutory interest in the property. For a lender to have a first lien on the property, the signature of the spouse is required to bind their statutory interest. Thus, marital status is an important issue, but only at the time of the closing, otherwise it is irrelevant.

When seeking legal advice, frequently the parties contact the attorney too late to address the important issues in the transaction. Buyers often decide an attorney is important to guide them through the closing process, after they have signed the contract. The trap for the unwary is that the attorney retained after the contract is already signed can often do little more than oversee the closing process to be sure it is handled in accordance with the terms of the contract and applicable state laws. Any changes an attorney might otherwise suggest may be precluded by the terms of the existing agreement. While the retention of an attorney is a step in the right direction, the time to do so is best before the contract is signed.

While it is noble that the developer or real estate agent suggests that taking the signed contract to an attorney, the recommendation should be made after the contract is prepared, but before it is signed. In fact, the best practice for a seller is to retain an attorney before even signing a listing agreement with a real estate company. The simple rule is sign nothing without attorney review to consider all pertinent, unique personal circumstances. While an attorney certainly can help after the listing agreement or contract is signed, one may not be taking maximum advantage of their ability to apply the law of the state where the property is located to the unique personal and financial circumstances or help negotiate the terms most favorable in light of those special needs.

Seek legal counsel before signing any legal document relating to a real estate transaction, no matter whether a buyer or seller. The stakes are too high in a real estate sale or purchase not to seek professional assistance. Each transaction is a unique event and should be handled as such since all facts and circumstances may not be readily apparent, and any one may cause unanticipated consequences. Remember also, no attorney can read your mind. They will not know specific personal or financial circumstances, desires, goals or conditions that are important unless they are informed of them. The more the attorney knows, the better they will be able to assist in the transaction. Remember, the reason for seeking legal help is to maximize the ability to achieve desired objectives in light of the law and personal circumstances. For example:

> *James T. Rowe and Janet D. Rowe, husband and wife, sign a listing agreement to sell their home. In reality, they know that if their son loses his job in the city, he will move in with them. In which case, he would like to move back into his old room. In this case, they would not want to sell their existing home. If they sign a listing agreement and the real estate agent finds a buyer pursuant to the terms of the sellers, the real estate agent may be due a commission even when they want to withdraw the property from the market.*

This precondition must be added into the listing agreement, or, the better alternative is the sellers should wait before listing the property. Any belief that they have no obligation to pay the commission if they did not go through with the sale could be costly. The proper course of action would be to discuss any preconditions with an attorney before signing a listing agreement.

This simple example illustrates one of the dangers in the real estate transaction. The assumption of knowing the applicable law or failure to realize that certain laws may govern the transaction may cause unanticipated, undesired consequences. The buyers who represent themselves armed only with their preconceptions are often in for a rude awakening. Unfortunately, the parties often assume others such as the real estate agents, friends or others who prepare the documents, will look out for their interests when, in fact, no such obligation exists. The only person who is going to look out for one's interests is the one in the mirror and those specifically hired to represent them.

The next area of danger concerns the sellers on a contract. The sellers on the contract are all those persons who have an interest in the property. This information may be trickier to disclose than it first appears, because without a title search to find the true owner(s) of record, the true status of the property is unknown. Due to the variation in statutes from state to state, the interests of non-owner spouses are determined by state law. These factors must be included in the analysis of the proper parties to the contract.

The greatest danger lies with the existence of non-owner spouses who are usually not disclosed in the public records, and must be determined from an analysis of the facts and circumstances involving the property. Remember, the simple rule that non-owner spouses who have statutory interests must be parties to the contract even though they do not appear in the public records. Occasionally, one may hear a woman say:

> *What I fear the most is that my husband will sell the house out from under me, take the proceeds and disappear leaving me with no where to go.*

If the woman is an owner, her husband cannot sell the property without her signature on the contract, the deed, and any other closing documents. The decision as to what marriage means to her will be important when she is asked to sign any document concerning property where she has any interest. Even if she agrees to sign, she needs to be aware that the closing agent is going to have the proceeds check prepared in the names of both sellers. Closing agents will refuse to be embroiled in any effort to have the proceeds disbursed in any other way.

Thus, the issue of how the proceeds are to be divided will still have to be dealt with after the closing because the proceeds check will simply list all the sellers. Division of the proceeds will depend on what marriage means to the sellers and the degree to which the old culture bias affects their social orientation. Disbursement of funds may be very tricky to negotiate if the sale of the property is related to a divorce action.

If the woman's interest is that of a non-owner spouse, she should seek the advise of an attorney in the state where the property is located to review her rights and the best way to protect those rights. As a cautionary note, a non-owner spouse should not move out of the family home before a sale or divorce without first obtaining legal advice. The rights of non-owners spouses vary from state to state and often are tied to possession. There are many issues in a real estate transaction, and contracts are lengthy in order to specifically address each of them. Because the old culture dangers do not appear in all aspects of a contract, the focus here is on the aspects where the old culture danger is likely to appear. However, another part of the real estate transaction deserves attention here. Watch for phrases like the following, which pose a special danger:

> *As seller I'll take care of the broken fence...*

If the obligation to repair the fence at seller's expense is not in the contract, the seller is not bound by any oral representation. Beware that old culture males are likely to enter into handshake agreements about the castle to show that they are living up to the image of the knight. In real estate transactions, these agreements are not enforceable, and often break down when the reality of the financial cost of the agreement is disclosed. A simple and wise rule to follow is to precisely spell out all aspects of the agreement in the written contract. The financial stakes in real estate transactions are too great to allow old culture biases, habits and customs to dictate the activities during the purchase and sale process.

When discussing the parties to the transaction, often one of the most important categories of people in our lives are omitted as a possible party. This oversight illustrates one of the unique dangers that have arisen out of the revolution; the failure to look out for the significant others in our lives. For the purposes here, the term "significant other" means those persons who are close to us spiritually and emotionally but are not tied to us by blood, marriage or adoption, or other legally recognized tie. The concept of "significant other" is dramatically illustrated by the following example:

> *Harry and Alice lived in an apartment together. Neither owned a house or property. Both were well along in years. Their relationship began as friends, but over time evolved so that she invited him to move in with her. To maintain her coverage through her deceased husband's medical plan, they never married. They had lived together for twelve years. The relationship was held together solely by love and affection.*
>
> *Alice became terminally ill, so Harry took care of her until her death. When she was admitted to the hospital as terminally ill, he was listed on the admission forms as the "significant other," a category used by the hospital to list the one to contact in an emergency. As a result of the revolution, this category substantially increased in importance to include persons not related by blood or marriage, but having status at the hospital. Harry visited her every day, and was accessible by phone when he was away from the hospital.*
>
> *All of Alice's legal and blood relatives lived several hundred miles away. She had very little contact with them. On the other hand, Harry only missed visitation six days during her last year*

in the hospital, and was at her bedside holding her hand when she passed.

When he called her nearest relatives to inform them of her death, suddenly, everything changed. They all arrived in force. He hardly knew any of them, but all of them were related by blood or marriage.

The relatives took over quickly. They made all the arrangements. They selected the funeral home, the casket, the cemetery and the service, where they spoke at length in her memory. At the service, Harry sat alone, a solitary figure in the back row of the pews in the church, tears rolling down his cheeks.

Immediately after the funeral service, Harry was asked to move out of her apartment as quickly as possible so they could sort through her things and clean out the apartment. They told him they wanted to wrap things up quickly so they could cancel the lease and go home.

In the American Dark Ages, back before the social revolution, the traditional family consisted of households consisting of husband, wife, and their biological children. Occasionally, the home also sheltered an in-law or two, but our society primarily consisted of the traditional biological family up to the end of the American Dark Ages. At the height of this period, the traditional family represented over 90% of the households in the country. All of our laws, government rules, and business organizations were structured around this old culture concept of the family. As society went through the social revolution, the world changed dramatically. Now, the traditional family makes up less than 30% of all households and the percentage is still dropping. However, contrary to the face of change, society and major institutions have continued to embrace the old culture definition of family with the entire fabric of all our business institutions remaining tied into what is now an increasingly unrealistic approach to the real world. The old culture images that motivated the adoption of the traditional family as the center of our society are also responsible for the powerful resistance to change that keeps the old culture concept of family locked firmly in place, even after the revolution. Today, the traditional family exists as a minority of family groups in our society.

The world is changing rapidly. There are signs that new domestic partner legislation in some states may begin to recognize the reality of the revolution, but the total ramifications of the social revolution are impossible to predict. On our journey to heightened awareness, simply be aware that the revolution has already brought many fundamental changes to our society. These changes to society will continue with the recognition of the modification of "family" lagging far behind for workable revisions in business and institutions. The current changes in the make up of the American household have made the old definition of "family" out of date. While the new domestic household often includes adult children, their offspring, and other blood relatives, in some cases it also includes significant others, those not related by blood or marriage.

Only after the beginning of the social revolution, the category of the significant other began to have real meaning as their numbers dramatically grew in size and recognition. This category has now reached a level that certainly justifies the label of "significant" and more than justifies serious attention to increase awareness of the world after the revolution. The following example appears to be becoming representative for more and more the population in our society today:

> *I did not like living alone. I ran an ad for a roommate when my boyfriend of several years left. Sandy was a divorcee who had adopted a young daughter on her own. We have become close friends over the last five years. My parents and my brother and his family live their own lives and are located in distant cities across the country. One day it dawned on me that Sandy and her daughter are my family. If something happens to me I want Sandy and her daughter to have this small house I own in my own name. They are the significant others in my life.*

It is increasingly likely that over the course of a lifetime, one individual will become involved with one or more other individuals with whom he or she becomes emotionally or spiritually close. These persons are ones closest to them and are cherished and cared for, yet are not legally related. For this reason, it is all too easy to overlook the fact that these people are not related in the old culture sense by blood, marriage, or legal adoption. There are currently no legally recognized relationships for significant others, even though they play the most important role in our lives on a daily basis. Significant others face a very different struggle than women who had to struggle with the anti-female cultural bias. Where, in most cases, husbands and wives have a recognized legal status, *significant others* do not.

Women have ECOA on their side to directly challenge culture in their struggle to gain access to credit; significant others face huge barriers in government, business and society against the adoption of the new culture to the extent it denies them recognition for *all* purposes. In addition, there is no champion on their side in their struggle against culture. They remain legally unseen. Although there are a few states that have introduced domestic partner legislation that is aimed at changing the existing old culture bias against significant others, this is a difficult barrier due to sexual bias against same sex partners whether actually engaging in homosexual behavior or just cohabiting as a financial relationship. Not surprisingly, the old culture images still control our lives, and to a large extent society does not recognize these people, who may be even more important to us than family. This failure is not due to the accident of birth, but due to choices made to include them as a part of our lives. Our culture does not acknowledge that our bond to them may be just as strong, or even stronger, than relationships created by birth, blood, or marriage.

For those born after the American Dark Ages where living together is increasingly common without formal legal ties, the danger exists for these special people who are called invitees, house guests, roommates, domestic partners, or just friends who will be overlooked in the areas legally significantly and important. The important point here is that there is a shared, special emotional or spiritual bond with them. In fact, they are often the most important people in our lives. As long as the old culture bias in society does not recognize these special people, and our laws that codified the old culture are blind to their existence and they have no protection unless specifically provided for in a legal, written document. The danger here is twofold. First, they are not included in our laws on descent and have no protection as an heir under the law of the land. The business community and government agencies do not recognize them as related to us for the purposes of social programs, medical insurance, retirement benefit plans, pensions, social security, or other programs. The second, and even more horrifying part of the danger is that more frequently in these relationships, when legalities arise, their partner has also overlooked them. Too often they are there for their partner in the hours of need, but are completely overlooked when the other partner dies. Too frequently, neither partner has taken the time to legally care for their significant other when the issue of legalities and death arise. For example:

> *Sandy owns a condominium unit in her own name. Marie and Sandy live in the unit. Sandy's only living relative is Aunt Mildred. When Sandy died suddenly and unexpectedly without*

> *a will, Marie, her partner, receives nothing through the estate. Aunt Mildred, Sandy's only living relative, whom she hated and never saw or spoke to, receives the condominium unit. Marie must move out and find a new life and living quarters elsewhere.*

The problem is the failure to provide for significant others in the same way as is done for legal, blood relatives. Unfortunately, most people often live their lives in this world automatically through the old culture bias. All else is ignored even though most believe they are transitional and sensitive to the individual human needs of their loved ones. In reality, most people are often not as transitional as they would like to think and believe. Since the revolution, significant others have become a new class of citizens, related to us solely by love and affection. Unfortunately, this new class of citizens may also be a class lower than second-class citizens. Many families consist of children being cared for by adults who are not related by blood, marriage, or adoption. Many people in our society are now living with persons who are not married. Those individuals who are involved in such relationships, whether same sex or heterosexual relationships, should be placed on notice that if something happens to one of these special people, the other will find that the old culture concepts of family relationship rule supreme legally to the extent that significant others are reduced to total insignificance.

Blood relatives are not alone in failing to consider the rights of significant others and persons who are related to us by love and affection when we die. The danger is that those of us who have such relationships are often the ones who fail to look out for the important people in their lives. If one owns a home and wants the person that is cohabiting in the home to have title to the castle if something happens to the owner, there are only two options available. Either one conveys an interest to them while still alive, or provide for them in a will. Otherwise they are left out in the cold, legally. For example:

> *Sarah Smith is not married and buys a property in her own name. She applies for and is approved for the mortgage loan in her own name.*
>
> *A year later, Sarah's boyfriend moved in and they lived together for two years. When she decides he is her significant other, she executes a deed to him of an undivided one half interest in the property as tenant in common.*

Adam's Eve

Later when they separate, he still has his undivided one half interest for which he has paid nothing. In addition, he is not obligated to pay the mortgage payments because he did not sign the mortgage note or assume the obligation to repay it.

Because a will can be changed at any time while alive, this vehicle legally provides flexibility over the deed which is effective when executed and recorded. The will provides the author the ability to react to a change in relationships. However, be forewarned that a will can be challenged in court on the basis of improper execution or undue influence. If one decides to use a will, be sure it is executed according to the laws of the state where it is effective.

New definitions are needed for our society. Until we replace the term "family" with a new term such as "extended family," "household," "domestic partner," "significant other" or some legally accepted terminology, or we adopt a special new legal definition of "family" to include significant others, these very important people will continue to be left out of our legal system. Even with a new definition to correct the present inequities, our society needs to change its basic structure that remains totally focused on the old culture definition of family to react to the realities now in practice.

The deed and will are the only tools legally available to protect those attached to people by emotion alone. Awareness of this situation is part of the journey to increased awareness. Life in the Transition includes taking responsibility for those one loves who are not legally related. Emotional attachment and commitment involves moral responsibility. Only those individuals involved in the relationships can act to protect the significant others in his or her life. No one else will do it, least of all current culture, business or government.

Another old culture term that will be either replaced or redefined as a result of the social revolution is "success." In the American Dark Ages when old culture males dominated the business world, "success" meant only two things. The first element of success for the individual in the American Dark Ages was achievement of a high level of authority in the pyramid structure of the organization in which the person was employed. The second element of success demanded achievement of commanding a level of monetary income significantly higher when compared to the other employees in the organization. The definition of success for the individual included only those who had commanded money and power above most of the others in the business organization. Many families in the American Dark Ages paid a high price to support the breadwinner husband in his quest for both these qualifiers for success.

The revolution has brought with it changes to our society, many of which are readily observable today. It will also bring many more changes that are just now becoming apparent. One of the differences destined for our society is how we define "success." In general, transitional men and women bring a different perspective and value system to the business organization than old culture male of the American Dark Ages. Transitional men are not as concerned about the concept of direct power. Nor are they as focused on income as a key determinant of success. Women are not buying into the traditional value system of the American Dark Ages but continually redefine their roles in relation to other women, men and children they bring into the world. Transitional people think more in terms of personal self-worth, social contribution, and value. This difference from the old culture bias may produce an alternative social approach to the employment environment. As transitional people climb the corporate ladder, they will bring a new perspective that includes a broader picture of life than the old culture male. First, they have objectives and goals that go beyond the employment environment, and work is only part of their lives. In addition, their new perspective will bring a new business approach to such things as:

On site day care facilities.
A redefinition of excused family time.
More flexible work schedules
Career growth without excessive travel and relocation
Increase in home based businesses or workstations
Increased family visitation to the workplace and/or involvement in home based businesses
Better access to affordable medical coverage.
Increased use of the Internet for the availability of work opportunities

Many other as yet unseen changes will also take place in the business environment as transitionals reach senior management positions. The net effect of these long-range changes including the re-definition of success will actually strengthen the traditional family and benefit children. In some cases, children coming up through the new educational systems and learning new technologies will increasingly contribute to accelerating the changes in society and our culture. In reality, children are actual or implied parties to every transaction. In the past, they were often left out because they were not yet seen as adults as defined by state law, and not legally responsible for their actions. If children own property, they need a legal guardian to manage it for them until they reach the age of majority. However, the old culture bias buried in our subconscious causes, in many ways, children to suffer from its narrow thinking and limited horizons.

When talking to a housewife married with two children, one might wonder how she sees herself in the Transition. She is likely to deflect every effort to inquire about herself. Ultimately, one realizes that in her own mind, she does not exist as an individual separate from her spouse and children. However, she may be inclined to defend her position as another example of the success of the old culture female who has successfully merged into the male and has no separate existence. With current awareness of the power of the old culture bias, one might realize she represents a serious issue which has been overlooked up to this point: children.

Transitional people tend to avoid the use of wife and husband because they carry old culture possessory connotations of objects rather than people. While transitional people may go to great lengths to refer to their spouses by name rather than possessory use of husband or wife, they often act instinctively in the use of the term *children* or *the kids* reacting the same way as old culture people. To both old culture males and females, children are seen the same way as they see wives and husbands. In fact, while children are not a direct part of the image of the knight and his princess on the way to the castle, the children are part of the future. In addition to being unseen, children are automatically thought of as objects and possessions just like a spouse. How many times have you heard a little girl say:

> *When I grow up, I want a house, a husband, a cat, and two babies of my own.*

People are not born transitional. They evolve through increased awareness of the restrictions and dangers of the old culture orientation, and they gradually learn to reject the fabled images over a period of time. For some unknown reason, one of the last clinging characteristics of old culture thinking is that of seeing children as possessions, much like the cat, the house, and the family car. This is often not done intentionally, but is the net result of actions taken towards children automatically without thought.

The failure to see children as separate unique human beings carries two dangers. One danger is to the children, but the other one is to the parent. The woman housewife is actually a good example of both these dangers. The world is changing so fast that by the time a woman is ready to teach her children about the outside world, her knowledge and training are seriously out of date. Increasingly, she must rely on teachers, coaches, counselors, and others to keep her knowledge and perspective current. The more she holds her children back to protect them, the more she intervenes and dominates their lives, and the greater the risk of long term damage to their ability to survive in the world outside the home when they are on their own years later. Adults, unfortunately suffer from the paradigm of growing old and gradually becoming disconnected from the reality of the younger generations. Their information comes from the time when they were coming up. The danger of the failure to see children as separate individual human beings at an early age is that it is easy for adults to live their lives through them where the adults influence them to do things that solved the adults' own unfinished needs more than answering theirs. Sometimes it is difficult for adults to realize that they do not own their children and are simply a custodian charged with the responsibility to bring them up. This way of thinking is part of what makes an individual transitional. For example:

> *Unless society outlaws the words baby and child and substitutes the term human being for both, most young women will not be induced to change the way they think. To most young mothers, children will always be seen as possessions when they are very young.*

There may be some set age when a child must be thought of as a person to avoid damage to their long-range growth. But because children are unique and we are all separate individuals, it is unlikely we will ever reach a consensus on an arbitrary date to determine their individual separateness. As a result, we will have to limit ourselves to drawing attention to the need to be aware of the danger of waiting too long. Thinking in terms of children as separate from parents or family at a certain age of maturity and recognizing the need to guide them to adulthood, parents will have developed the awareness of the different needs, desires, and interests of each individual, separate child.

Undoubtedly, many have seen bumper stickers some parents display on the back of family cars that announce the academic accomplishments of a child. Unfortunately, the bumper stickers are not placed there for lauding the child or the peers of the child because the children don't drive the cars. The sticker is the announcement by the parent to other adults of the success of the parent having a child who achieves good grades and is thereby a successful, good parent. These bumper stickers are good examples of the parent living through the child and taking credit for the accomplishments of the child as their own. As custodian of a child, parents should be proud of their child's independent accomplishments. The success in school is that of the child, not the parent. Good grades and special recognition by the school are the most important things to the child, and help the child develop a healthy independent life. It is important that parents don't steal the child's success and make it their own. The bumper stickers are only an announcement of the old culture status of the parent. The parent with issues will announce the fantastic accomplishments of "their child," as validating them as a successful parent.

To avoid falling into the trap of living life through their children, adults must maintain a life independent from them. An adult has no right to obtain personal gratification and emotional needs through the lives of others, and certainly not from their children. This represents a particular form of abuse to the child. In the modern world of today, parents must turn their children loose to learn how to cope beyond the control of the adult as soon as possible. The world is changing too fast. Only the ones struggling in it can keep up with the constant changes and learn how to keep up with them successfully. Parents owe their children the best chance possible for success in the outside world by taking the first step to set them free. Parents will not help them when unaware of the danger of living their lives through their children.

Parents who decide that it makes sense to convey the beach house to their children face two dangers. First, they may be looking at their children as possessions not seeing the individual differences between them. One of the children may be ideally suited to handle property, while another is far too immature or not even interested. Secondly, children are often thought of like the old culture images, frozen in time. Parents often see them at certain ages and cannot visualize them grown up with children of their own. Thus, conveying the beach house to the children may appear to be the right thing to do, but if children are thought of as separate unique human beings with their own families in the not so distant future, what seemed like the right thing to do may in fact be totally wrong. Adults need to look at each child as a unique human being and not as stereotyped objects.

The woman housewife with two children cannot tell you about herself because in a very real sense she does not exist. She only lives through others, following what she thinks she is supposed to do, letting the old images dictate her life. She is living to help her husband, her family and her children. The greatest old culture danger for both men and women as unique separate individuals is that they give up their personal goals, dreams, and aspirations when they marry. Immediately, they begin sacrificing their lives for the sake of the old culture images. What makes human beings unique is that we gain our greatest happiness and personal satisfaction in the enjoyment of seeking personal goals and dreams. Just as the solitary life in the castle is a total denial of this goal for females, so too is the sacrifice of personal dreams and aspirations for the sake of children. It is equally wrong for a parent as it is wrong for the children to replace one's own dreams with theirs. Just as children need to establish their own independent lives, so must the parent. Living a rich and fulfilling personal life is the best example parents can set as a transitional custodian for their children.

The danger to the parent is strongest when their objective in life is simply to live the old culture lifestyle because it means sacrificing all personal goals. The power of the old culture myth is that it creates the most danger to both adults and children. Special problems arise in divorced families. The children are often not considered when contemplating a second marriage. Are children asked which last name they want, that of their biological father or that of your new spouse? The question is just as valid for them as it is for the parent. In addition, do they have the maturity to understand the real implications of the decision? Any adult that considers asking the children what they desire indicates recognition by the parent that the child is an individual human being. In such case it is unlikely the parent is living their life through them. Still, it is important to be careful what you do and say. Children are watching every act a parent makes and listens to every word the parent says. Children hear even what is not said.

How many times have parents stated they held their marriage together for the sake of their children, or at least until the children are grown. This sounds like a noble act of extreme sacrifice, but it is usually the opposite for both the parents and their children. When parents think of their children as possessions, they do not see how much their children know at an early age. They fail to see that their own marital difficulties are apparent to their children. The solution that seems so noble is often a lesson to the children that their parent's relationship is the best that life has to offer. This is a disservice to children who are likely to grow up and repeat the same lifestyle.

Dealing with the truth instead of hiding in an artificial stereotype lifestyle is the core of what it means to be transitional. If adults recognize children as human beings, they will discover that they can handle the truth much better than anticipated. Sometimes adults can go too far in the zeal to recognize children as individual human beings. For example:

> *As a single parent I want my six-year-old daughter to inherit my home. I want to add her name on the deed to avoid the costs of probate.*

Certainly, it is possible in most states to execute a deed of an interest in property to a minor child. However, the problem is that any child under the age of majority as defined by state law doesn't have the legal capacity to enter into a contract, or any other agreement, and any action they take is not binding on them. Even though a parent is the natural guardian of their own children, in most states a parent cannot act for their children in matters over a certain limit in value. And almost universally, a parent cannot act as natural guardians for their children where real estate is involved. Thus a formal guardianship must be set up with all acts subject to supervision of the court. A guardian will be bound to do only those things that are in the best interest of the child, a standard many parents find more difficult than their own. There are significant costs involved in setting up and administering a formal guardianship, so the woman's desire to avoid the expense of probating her estate is not rational because the cost of a guardianship may be even greater.

Children are not considered significant others because they are related by blood. In fact, in most states if a parent dies leaving no spouse and only children, those children will inherit the entire estate. As long as the distribution of assets as provided by the state according to inheritance laws, one does not need a deed or a will to provide for their children. Simply because no one can predict the future, maintaining flexibility is usually the better practice when it comes to owning real estate. Thus, keeping the title to property in one's own name is usually the preferred means to maximize one's options. Another good rule is to avoid transferring title to children whether they are minors or adults until one is sure to never need the property back under any circumstances. The advantage of inheritance laws and the use of a will is that they do not become effective until death, leaving maximum flexibility to deal with property while the owner is still living. Keep in mind one needs to discuss plans with an attorney who specializes in elder law when one reaches fifty-five as soon as feasible.

Living a full rewarding life for oneself, including the use of property, is the best way to prepare children for a life on their own in the real world. Adults who demonstrate to their children they have an independent life, separate and apart from the children, are the best example a parent can set for them.

CHAPTER THIRTEEN: A MATTER OF TRUST

While there are both old culture men and women, there is one particular characteristic of old culture men one needs to be especially aware of. One of the easiest ways to detect the old culture male is to listen for his response, "Trust me" in answer to a legitimate question. We all know that when an old culture male drives a car and is obviously not going the correct or easiest way to reach a destination, and his spouse or female companion suggests that he pull over and ask for directions often the response is:

"Trust me. I know what I'm doing."

Even if the woman is one of the lucky few who can lure him to pull over and seek assistance, she might follow up by asking:

"Did you get directions?"

His response once again is likely to be,

"Trust me."

Chances are he didn't pay any attention to any instructions he received and he merely stopped to get her off his back and seek help from another male. Often when this happens, the woman is in deep trouble for challenging him. As a general rule, old culture males do not stop and ask for directions. The reason for this behavior can be easily explained in terms of the old culture image of the knight in shining armor. Knights who are out riding their loyal steeds never ask serfs of the village for directions. As a knight, the appearance of knowing what he is doing is often far more important than actually having the knowledge. To allow a lowly serf discover that a knight does not know what he is doing is to totally lose face. This action is an unforgivable sin for a knight. In addition, the knight would rather lose face with a serf than with his princess. He *always* knows better than his princess. If the princess volunteers travel information, the knight is likely to either do precisely the opposite or simply ignore her. If his response is silence, this response can also be substituted for "Trust me." The general rule to remember is that a knight never accepts instructions from anyone, especially from his princess.

In addition, knights also know that if someone asks for directions, he must provide a best guess rather than admit not to know. This is part of the reason knights don't stop and ask for directions. A knight must never admit he doesn't know the answer. The "Trust me" response is one way to avoid such an admission. However, the response is only used when his pauper princess asks a knight a direct question, or he is silent. The response is never used when dealing with other knights or outsiders.

This book is about castles and not rides in the countryside on a Sunday afternoon. An awareness of the reasons for the use of the "Trust me" response is important because the purchase of the family home is the most common situation where it will be used. To the old culture male, the residence is the castle in his fantasy image and is an integral part of his self-perception. For this reason, the process of acquisition of the castle is the domain of the knight as lord and master of his realm. The following is a common response by a woman to the use of her knight's "Trust me" response concerning questions about the purchase of their home:

> *I hate it when I ask him a question and he answers, "Trust me." What he means is that I am supposed to shut up and be quiet. He is saying that he is in charge, and he will make all the decisions. He is implying that if he wants my opinion or input in any way, he will ask for it, which of course he never does.*

The response, "Trust me," is likely to mean one or more of the following:

1. Do not criticize anything I do.
2. You don't appreciate what I have done for you.
3. I know more than you do.
4. You're blaming me for everything.
5. I know what I'm doing.
6. It's my job to take care of the house closing.

7. Don't you question what I'm doing about the castle.

Of course, all too often the old culture male doesn't have the answer to the question asked and simply refuses to admit it. The above list is representative of what the response often means, but it is by no means complete. However, the list helps translate what the knight usually means when he says, "Trust me." The greatest danger is for the unwary to ignore the red flag raised by this response. For a female to continue to pursue an issue after hearing the "Trust me" response is to tread on dangerous waters. She could be threatening the very core of her marital relationship. A woman may not know what marriage means to her, but the old culture male knows exactly what it means to him.

Notice that none of the above responses even acknowledges the validity or applicability of the original question. The response simply deflects the effort to raise the issue. In real estate transactions, the economic impact of any questions is of no concern to the old culture male when his dominion and control over anything to do with the castle is challenged. For example:

> *The contract is prepared with the buyer given certain inspection rights before closing. If an inspection is made pursuant to the contract and it reveals repairs covered by the contract are needed, the seller has the obligation to make the repairs.*
>
> *The seller approaches the buyer after the contract is signed and offers to lower the purchase price by the sum of $1,000.00 if the buyer will waive the inspection right. The buyer brings the amendment to the contract to his wife for her signature. When she questions the change, he says, "Trust me."*
>
> *She signs the amendment. Then they obtain a building inspection. The report states a new roof is required at a cost of $6,000.00. Their bank refuses the mortgage loan unless the work is done, which has to be paid by the buyers because the seller's obligation for repairs was deleted in the amendment.*

The wife's reliance on the knight's "Trust me" response cost the buyers $5,000.00. Remember, the old culture individual's need to reinforce and support the image is more important than economics. The need for the old culture male to appear that he knows what he is doing is more important when dealing with the castle than at any other time. Sometimes when asked a question, the knight will mumble or garble the response in such a way that it is impossible to understand his response. The objective of this type of response is to induce the listener to interpret it to mean whatever they want. This is also a deliberate tactic for the knight. The listener is usually too embarrassed to ask for the response to be repeated clearly. When the answer is garbled, it is the equivalent of the "Trust me" response. In addition, if there is no doubt the question has been heard and there is *no answer*, remember that silence is also the equivalent of the "Trust me" response. Too many times people hope for the best and misinterpret the garbled response or silence to mean there is agreement between the parties. Such responses are often construed as a confirmation when in fact these responses mean exactly the opposite. Actually, silence generally means the knight considers that the question is not even worthy of a response. If the one to whom the question is addressed is old culture, then everyone should *know* his or her answer. The one addressed often feels it is ridiculous to even respond to the obvious, so they say nothing at all. The knight feels that the question is a stupid question because the answer is obvious.

The danger here is not in the way they handle the question but in the subsequent interpretation of their reaction. The "Trust me" response is also used when questions are centered on the issue of extramarital affairs. The knight's self-protective response is usually to counter the question with a question, such as:

Don't you trust me?

The answer, of course, is no. Old culture men see their wives as objects. Thus, they are free to have extramarital affairs because they are not hurting anyone. Extra marital affairs are not uncommon with old culture males, and the above response is a clear indication an affair is taking place. On the other hand, old culture females are often jealous and suspicious because they are using their husbands the same way their husbands are using them. Each see the other simply as a means to reach the objective of a lifestyle modeled in the old culture images. As a result, cross suspicions and marital distrust are common and often justified.

One of the most important cornerstones of the marriage relationship is trust. In fact, the concept of trust is absolutely crucial for a good marriage. However, real trust is something that must be earned over time. More frequently, the essential trust has not been earned but is demanded by the "Trust me" response. When there is a demand for trust, this behavior is a warning that all is not well at a fundamental level in the relationship. If real trust existed, the response would not be necessary. The internal self-perception of the male as the knight in shining armor riding on his trusty steed ready to protect his domain looks at any challenge to control of the castle as a personal attack that must be met by a counter challenge. This fantasy is all too often an irrational and emotional one, with the "Trust me" response as the most frequent.

To avoid serious conflicts, a wife must be submissive and trusting of her husband's decision making when it comes to issues involving the castle. However, as in our example, the issues can be raised in the privacy of home in advance. All questions involving the castle must be handled in a delicate manner as we have intimated.

In real estate transactions, the woman can overcome any anticipated resistance at the closing by ordering copies of all the closing documents in advance. Once the documents are available, the buyers can review them and ask all questions well before the closing. If the only response is an irrational answer, she can pursue the matter and ask further questions before any financial damage is done. Remember, there is a wrong way and wrong time to raise questions if the male is old culture.

Notwithstanding the risks of treading on dangerous waters, either party needs to review the issues since the home is the single most important asset anyone is likely to own during their lifetime. Even if there is little equity when purchased, over time, real estate will increase in value due to the ever-increasing population pressure. The financial significance to both parties continues to grow over the years. Every question needs to be addressed, and each individual has the right to ask them.

Another point to remember is that the old culture male does not want an attorney to represent him at the closing. He will claim it costs too much money, but often his real reason is that the appearance of an attorney diminishes his role as the knight in front of others. For this reason many buyers may not have an attorney present on their behalf. Having a pre-closing legal review is one way to address male resistance to hiring an attorney at closing and a good time to have questions answered by a professional.

Whenever a spouse hears the "Trust me" response from their partner, beware. This is a warning that should not be ignored. The verbal expression of the words "Trust me" is notice to reevaluate the relationship with that person. For a woman already in a marriage who has not been aware of the different social orientations, her marriage may be difficult to maintain. A high degree of awareness on her part along with good negotiating skills will be required to hold such a marriage together once she detects that her own social orientation is changing while his is not. Beware that willingness to accept the "Trust me" response can quickly become an adoption of old culture thinking and become a trap far beyond any expectations.

Those who think lightly of the serious nature of the differences in social orientation as evidenced by the "Trust me" response need to study the many cases of husbands who have killed their wives. Cases where women have killed their husbands disclose motivations inspired by the discovery of another love partner or pure financial greed, but the husband who kills his wife often expresses his motivation as:

> *No one understands. I simply could not let her go. If I can't have her for myself, no one else can have her. I'll make sure of that.*

The male who kills his wife often shows no outside love interest, no economic motive, just a need to preserve his old culture identity as lord and master of his domain. Old culture males simply do not see their wives as separate, equal human beings; no matter how charming and caring they may seem during the courtship. The primary need in life for the old culture male is to use marriage to fulfill an internal image and make poor Adam whole again. If the couple goes through a divorce, poor Adam is being torn apart once again. No old culture male can be a knight unless he has a princess. For this reason, divorce for the knight becomes a personally destructive event, far more damaging to males than to females.

The danger is that old culture males will go to great lengths to lure a potential mate into their old culture trap. All too often when he says, "I love you," he means, "I need you." What he really means is he needs to fulfill his internal image of himself, and he needs the princess to fulfill this need. There is no flexibility in the old culture male. Every unmarried female must be able to detect the social orientation of her suitors. Often the first clue of social orientation is in his use of the words, "Trust me."

If both spouses have an old culture orientation, their relationship may have the capacity to survive for some time. If both are transitional, chances are the relationship will flourish. On the other hand, if they each have different social orientations, their relationship most likely will not work. If a woman is old culture and starts to become transitional, her life is likely to become increasingly difficult at home. These mixed orientation households are the ones where violence against women has the greatest opportunity to occur. These are the relationships that keep the divorce statistics high. The increase in marital strife that takes place today arises because males and females do not reject the old culture images at the same time or at the same rate. Thus, husbands and wives grow farther apart, and the range of things they share decreases. As one spouse changes, the other remains the same. The quality of their marital life quickly deteriorates. Often the conflict swells to cause violence by the old culture male against his transitional wife. The male is hurt far more than the female. The divorce involves the loss of his personal identity, a part of himself, and that he cannot accept. For this reason, the mere threat of divorce is often the motivation behind domestic violence.

Females who become transitional while still in old culture marriages often realize the danger of the great divide and fear for their lives should they ever leave their old culture husbands. No one will ever know how many marriages are held together, not by love, but by fear. In addition, many old culture wives say they are caught by surprise when their husbands suddenly walk out of their marriages. Often, the husbands was becoming transitional and may even have tried to bring their wives along with them only to give up and leave when they saw no hope for change. Old culture people are usually totally unaware of the subtle outward indications that a person is changing. To them, all people are the same.

Awareness of the differences in social orientation in advance can save anguish and heartache. One of the primary awareness warning signs is to listen carefully to the answers to legitimate questions. If the response is either silence or "Trust me," be forewarned. Individuals with the old culture orientation reveal this attitude in response to financial matters, especially those relating to the home.

The same simple categorizations applied to domestic life can also be applied to the work environment. There are business organizations that are strictly old culture in orientation, just as there are corporations that can be described as transitional. However, unlike a spouse who will disclose social orientation through their responses as "Trust me," the orientation of a business is more difficult to discern.

Just as it is important to understand whether a prospective spouse is old culture before accepting a marriage proposal, so too is it important to decide whether a prospective employer also fits into the old culture category before accepting a career position. The purchase and maintenance of a castle is expensive and thus employment security is an important factor in the analysis of an employer for financial stability. People spend most of their lifetime in the work environment, so it is just as important to determine whether the environment is compatible with one's personal orientation as it is for a potential spouse. To purchase and maintain a castle, employment stability is essential. The employment trap may begin in the first job one accepts. Work experience often determines the career path and the general location where one will work and live for most of his/her life. The truth is that often the experience on one's first job transitions the opportunities available for the second job. One's career success depends on the experiences built from job to job, becoming the foundation of the employment trap. The scope and direction of most careers are determined by the first full time job accepted. To assure success in employment, it is extremely important to determine the nature of the social orientation that exists within the organization before accepting an employment offer.

The problem with accepting a job is the difficulty in determining the culture of an organization before accepting employment. When one discovers a true clash in orientation after accepting a position, the only solution ultimately is avoidance. An old culture organization is just like an old culture person, unable to change its ways. Isolated bias and prejudice exist everywhere, in a supervisor, other employees, or the head of the department. If the old culture bias exists in top management, beware. The president, board of directors, and senior officers of an organization set the culture for the entire organization. Their influence determines the direction of the organization. If the prevailing old culture orientation exists in the senior officers, it is highly likely the whole organization will have a culture that follows their leadership. Before accepting employment, it is difficult to determine the culture of the environment during the initial exposure. However, if one is careful and alert, detecting the orientation during the interview process is possible. Look for a means to detect the orientation during the interview. The objective is to find an indication whether the entire facility or company is old culture, not just one individual. During the interview, ask questions that are not directly related to the job description. Women can take the initiative and ask questions such as the following:

>   Ask questions about day care facilities.
>   Ask questions about maternity leave.
>   Ask questions about how the company handles harassment on the job.
>   Ask questions about personnel in upper management determine if there are significant numbers of females.
>   Ask questions about promotions and pay raises.
>   Ask questions about training and opportunities for changing positions.

The silence response in the employment interview will not occur, but watch for the garbled response, the clear misstatement, change of topic, and turning the question back to the interviewee. In each of these cases, be forewarned. As soon as one develops the skills to detect an old culture environment, one must decide whether they have the skills to survive in that environment. Ultimately, if there is a clash in orientation, the only solution will be to begin the process of seeking opportunities in another facility or organization. If the old culture bias dominates the interview process and this is unworkable, simply terminate the interview and politely leave the premises. If the old culture bias is acceptable for your social orientation, then the opportunity may work. Once again, if social orientations do not match, ultimately avoidance is essential. Remember that the enemy of employment success is culture, not personal, no matter whether the interviewer is male or female.

In the employment environment, the "Trust us" response is often more implicit rather than expressed. Unfortunately, the only way to totally and accurately determine the social orientation or culture of an organization is to actually work there. The employment danger is that the longer you stay in an employment environment, the more difficult it is to leave. The time to change jobs or career is when young and when the time invested is small in a non-productive job or career direction.

There is a second career or employment trap to be aware of. Many self-improvement books pitch a common theme that unless one's career goal is the number one position in the organization, every interim job must be a step in a direct path to achieve that goal. Failure to do so will cause misery, unhappiness, and even psychological depression. The reality is actually being number one is not for everyone. Such positions require special characteristics and dedication. As one builds working experience in an organization, it is important to be realistic and adjust goals as one sees how they fit in the organization. The important questions follow:

>   Do you really want to be number one?
>   Are you willing to make the personal sacrifices required?
>   Do you have the qualifications for the position?

In an organization of thousands of employees, there is only and can be only one number one. For happiness and success in life, everyone must seek what is right for him/herself as an individual, setting realistic goals for a position that best balances skills and desires. One must be true to him/herself when evaluating goals. Determining how much time to allocate for work and how much to other goals and interests is primary. The life of the president of an organization almost always involves a total personal sacrifice for the company with little time left for outside interests and desires.

Often negative connotations are assigned to those who do not unquestioningly adopt a career goal leading to the top position. Learn to avoid this trap and set a realistic agenda. Such generalities encountered in self-help books, encouraging everyone to seek the top positions, ignore the fact that everyone is very different. Failure to be realistic sets individuals up for unreasonable and unrealistic expectations. This can be one of the fastest ways to early burnout and career dissatisfaction. The only real question is whether the organization where one is employed has the interim jobs that will lead to the position that provides personal satisfaction. Does the company provide opportunities for advancement, training, and experiences that lead to that desired ideal position or will the old culture orientation of the organization block workers from achieving advancement goals?

The third employment trap to avoid is often stated in terms that money is everything and both the employee and the company must focus on that goal. The common work environment myth is that almost everything is controlled by economics. Again, this is not necessarily true. The first rule of every organization is not this year's bottom line, but its own self-preservation. Profits for any one year are often sacrificed for long-term maintenance of the status quo of the corporate culture. If economics were the sole determinant, there would be no hiring prejudice and the best-qualified person would always be selected for promotion. Discrimination exists when the best-qualified person is not selected due to a bias for something other than job qualifications. Many companies have gone out of business or wound up in bankruptcy because they failed to change the internal culture.

When preservation of the corporate or organizational culture overrides basic economic rules, avoid the organization. The old culture spouse will protect old culture values and internal self-images when dealing with the home to the extent that basic economics are ignored. Preservation of the old culture image becomes the overriding concern. The same behavior can be found in many business organizations.

Where a male and a female are equally qualified and the man is selected over the woman, there may be bias in the selection process, but it is not lethal to the corporation. When the female is clearly more qualified than the male, then preservation of the old culture image overrides the best economic interests of the company. The goal of the organization becomes preservation of the old culture. In such cases, avoidance is the only option. Any time preservation of the old culture prevails to the detriment of a human enterprise; no matter if it is a marriage or a large industrial corporation, immediate avoidance is the only alternative for the transitional person.

When accepting a job in a business organization, the basic rule is to trust no one. The second rule is to block opportunities for old culture prejudices to appear. Personal professionalism is the best way to keep old culture people at bay. Attitude and demeanor often determine the degree of old culture behavior encountered on the job. Fortunately, most professionalism is common sense; so just being aware of its power to counter old culture people can successfully keep the old culture bias at bay. Developing an independent and self-contained approach to the work place can be learned. This attitude involves creating the right personal image to offset the old culture that lies within all individuals and business organizations. In the war against culture in the workplace, if you must trust someone, learn to trust yourself.

CHAPTER FOURTEEN: CASTLES IN THE SAND

The basic premise here is that our culture has adopted the story of the creation of Eve from the tearing out of part of poor Adam's rib. By adopting the marriage ceremony into the culture, the celebration represents making poor Adam whole again by merging Eve back into Adam as one. This merger is underscored by the fact that women give up their identity in marriage by taking the the their husband's name, thus disappearing as separate individuals. In addition, the myth of the knight in shining armor who claims his princess by sweeping her off her feet and whisking her away on his mighty steed to live happily ever after in his castle augments the plight of the woman as a separate human being. In the myth, the knight takes his princess from a life of misery and poverty to the lofty heights of the castle where he protects and provides for her forever. Once consciously aware of these two images, one can apply them to become more aware of reality. Hopefully, this awareness will help individuals avoid automatically following old traditions and thought patterns that may work against personal and financial issues.

The old culture story of the marriage ceremony as the merger of the female back into the male demonstrates the importance of our names. Life for males in our society is relatively straightforward. Men have no major identity crisis. A man's name clearly defines who he is. The only rule to remember is to use the full name and avoid falling back on abbreviations or nicknames, and courtesy titles such as Dr., Doctor, Esquire, Esq., which are not a part of a legal name. However, sequence names such as Senior, Sr., Junior, Jr., II, III are a necessary part of the name, designating the person as separate from other persons in the family with the same name. For this reason, these sequence names must be used whenever possible.

For the male, there are only three reasons to change his name. First, if adopted when very young, adoptive parents will usually change the last name of the adopted son to that of the family name. Second, emigrants from foreign countries where the name is difficult to spell or pronounce will simplify the name as a convenience. Third, some men who are employed in high profile public life as in politics or the entertainment industry will sometimes change their names to increase the ease of market exposure.

One thing men will simply never do: they will not change their last names to that of their wife's family on marriage. Researching the issue to find a foundation for the strong resistance to what can only be described as a social taboo. The only answer is culture, attributable to the internal adoption of the two old culture images.

Women who do not marry are similar to men in their reasons for changing their last names. Adoption when young, simplification of a long and difficult name, and the search for ease in a higher market profile provide the same reasons for unmarried women as for men. However, for married women, the issues are quite different. Those coming from outside our culture may wonder why women change their names since name recognition is so important. There is no logical or legal answer to the question of why women give up their names so willingly in our society, other than it's culture. However, understanding our culture and awareness of the internal images explains why the practice is commonplace. The disappearance of the female name is simply an expression of the merger of the female back into the male to make poor Adam whole again. As a counter to our culture, ECOA sets out three credit options for married women:

> She can use her maiden name
> She can use her married name
> She can use a combination name

Under ECOA, no one can force a married woman to use one name to the exclusion of the others. The decision of which name to use is hers alone, and is reinforced by ECOA. When the old culture prevailed in the American Dark Ages, the practice of females changing their last names to that of their husbands went on generation after generation without thought. This traditional name change was done automatically, without question. Many people become visually upset when someone is brave enough to ask why. As a society, people simply followed the practice blindly, without thought. Before the social revolution, females were old culture and either stayed home as old culture housewives or took entry-level jobs where their names had no economic value. There was no reason not to follow the practice until the revolution when women began to have careers. As a result, name recognition for the female now became critical and had value. The revolution also brought with it the value of credit for women. It is no coincidence that the universal credit card became popular in the mid 1960's in the early years of the revolution. Suddenly, name recognition was important for women, just as it always had been for men. Beginning with the revolution, personal identity had financial value regardless of gender.

The social revolution changed everything. Careers and a credit ratings have replaced early marriage as the focus of young women in their twenties and thirties. Day to day economic reality changed the way women thought, and pushed them away from the old culture value system and into the untried world of the Transition. Economic reality will continue to push females away from the old culture that held them back from a world of opportunities. Because of the revolution, our society will never be the same, and simple economics will push more women to retain their birth names as the Transition progresses.

As transitional women have children, they appear to continue to give their children the last name of the biological father, if they legally marry him. If they don't formalize their relationship through marriage, often, young women fill in the birth certificate with their own last name and do not identify the father. The only pitfall of concern with such cases is that if they do not name the father on the birth certificate, they may be precluded legally from seeking child support from the biological father.

Beginning in the early days of the revolution, the role of father increasingly became a vanishing figure, and the number of homes without a biological father present grew dramatically. The reality of fatherless homes will continue as long as the historical forces that led to the revolution adversely affect men. Current statistics show that the percentage of traditional two parent families is at an all time low. In addition, transitional mothers will deliberately avoid old culture males. The number of conventional families will not increase as a percentage of total households until more males become transitional. Only time will disclose how our society will handle name identification as the population moves into a predominantly transitional orientation. As, females learn the importance of name recognition, and the dangers of multiple name use expand.

In the early days of female employment in the American Dark Ages, women took jobs that had no specific need for identity. Now, the higher level the position, the more important name recognition becomes, causing the old culture tradition of name change to decrease. Increased awareness in the Transition will also continue to push women towards a future away from the old culture concept of the merger of the female back into the male with its characteristic loss of separate female identity. The need for a separate credit identity will continue to increase the pressure on the old culture concept of name change.

Already, changes have occurred such as when people marry. The old culture designation of the couple as James T. Rowe and Mary Rowe, his wife is beginning to yield to new designations. New terminology such as "husband and wife" and "married to each other" have found their way into the ceremony just as the word "obey" has disappeared from the marriage ceremony. As one observant woman so clearly pointed out:

> *I bristle at the use of the words "his wife." When I hear that phrase, I hear "his wife and personal possession." Every female should be offended at the use of such language. You seldom hear of the phrase "Mary Rowe and John D. Rowe, her husband."*

Whenever the old culture prevails, she is right. Culture dictates that the husband's name is given first, when legally the order of names has no significance. Name use can be important and can lead to traps for the unwary. For example:

> *When I was very young, my grandfather bought me a certificate of deposit. Unfortunately, he had it issued to "Missy Richards." My real name is Roberta, but I have always been "Missy" to my friends and family. Today, I am married and my last name is Walters. When I tried to cash in the certificate, I had a real problem proving I was the real owner. I had to prove that my maiden name was Richards. Then I had to produce my birth certificate that showed my name as Roberta. I'm struggling with the problem that my name was given as "Missy" and not Roberta on the certificate. Frankly, I don't know when my ownership will be straightened out.*

The issue of name recognition will continue to be a problem for females until they learn to develop a property list and put all property in the one name and maintain that name as the one they use for all financial purposes. Another example of how names can trap the unwary is illustrated by the following example:

When I first got married, I took my husband's name. I didn't question it. I did what everyone else did. I went to work developing my career until both my friends and business associates recognized me by my married name.

When I got divorced, I found that I was better off keeping my married name. My birth given last name had no value. In fact, a restoration of my old name would only hurt me. I really wanted my first husband out of my life, but I would have been crazy not to keep the name by which everyone knew me.

I'm getting married again, but this time I've learned my lesson. I'm not going to change my name, even though it will put me in an awkward position. I will be in a marriage, keeping the name of a person I want nothing to do with. My name will remain that of my first husband and my new husband will have a different name than mine.

Sometimes the name game can be a benefit. The most important characteristic of an old culture male is the reaction to a statement by a woman who agrees to a marriage but wants to keep her own name. The response to her statement will be clear, firm, and totally predictable. The old culture male will insist, in no uncertain terms, that the female take his name and it is legally required that she do so. This is the simplest and easiest test to identify the old culture orientation in the male. Beware that the old culture male will often try hard to sweet talk his way into the life of the female he chooses to make poor Adam whole again. He will try to hide his old culture orientation until the marriage is consummated. However, the threat to maintain a maiden name will almost always elicit a response that gives him away. In reality, only the female can decide what name she will use. It is no one else's decision.

Name recognition is a core part of the old culture. Poor Adam cannot be made whole again without the merger of the female back into the male. This issue becomes one the old culture male cannot simply let go unchallenged. Her identity is not what is at issue; it is his. On the other hand, the transitional male simply won't care what name a woman uses. He is likely to be most supportive of whatever choice she makes because he cares about her as a person. A transitional male is interested in the personal growth and development of the person he marries. In fact, he is likely to prefer that she maintain her maiden name, because he is sensitive to the possessory implication of her use of his last name and the financial implications of a change in her name. A middle aged professional woman who owned her own business in her own name decided to enter into a second marriage:

> *I have spent years building my business. It bears my name to this day. I am not going to change my name just because I'm getting married again. I kept my name the first time and I'll keep it now. I'm not going to commit professional and financial suicide just because I'm getting married.*

She stands out, not because of her strong position reinforcing the previous examples, but because she quietly set a double standard. She dropped her middle name, but kept her original last name. She then simply used his last name when it was expedient in her personal life. Professionally, she simply used her birth name with which she had established and maintained her business. She was transitional, with economics as the force driving her away from the old culture restraints. She still uses his last name socially in her personal life, a tie to the old culture.

In the early 1970's, a very transitional married couple worked for different marketing-advertising agencies. As a result, they shared friends and business associates. When they decided to divorce, they knew their friends would feel caught between them, not knowing whose side to take. To address this problem, they came up with an ingenious and very transitional solution: they held a divorce party. They sent out invitations to all their common friends and business associates. They had a special cake made for the occasion, and they hired the ever-important photographer. The highlight of the party was when they stood behind the cake and cut out two pieces. Each picked up a piece and proceeded to splatter it directly into the other's face to the great amusement of all who attended. The all-important photographer fulfilled his mission by taking pictures of the dramatic cake exchange.

Copies of the photographs of this humorous event were circulated not just to those present but to everyone they knew who was unable to attend. This creative approach to the change in life circumstances broke the ice, and the mutual relationships were maintained. Divorce may have ended their intimate personal relationship, but they were true transitionals, making even divorce a civil and even humorous event among friends and business associates. For once, the old culture bias was nowhere to be seen. This couple understood that we live in a world of constantly changing relationships and alliances where our personal and business lives often overlap. They refused to allow the old stereotype behavior established back on the old subsistence farms to apply to their future successes.

One exasperated woman shared the following story:

> *All I wanted to do was to send out my annual holiday cards. It was as simple as that. Yet, now that I am aware some people are old culture and some are transitional, I felt I should be more sensitive than I had been last year when I addressed all my cards to:*

> Mr. Mrs. James T. Rowe and family

> *This year, I realized that some of my female friends are transitional. I was sure they must have been offended with my callous approach last year. I'm sure they had been telling me who they were for years, but I had not been paying attention to the differences in social orientation. I found myself dividing my cards into two groups. I continued addressing cards for the people I thought were still old culture the same way. I decided on a new approach for those I was sure are transitional:*

> James T. Rowe, Mary Jane Rowe and family

> *Then I realized some women would want their maiden names used instead of their married names. On top of that, I wondered if I should list the woman's name before her husband. I began to wish I had never gone to the seminar. Addressing holiday cards will never be the same.*

Now that we are well into the Transition, addressing holiday cards is not the only thing that is changing. In fact, virtually nothing in our social lives will ever be the same as it was before the revolution. Awareness of the power of old customs and practices gives us much to decide, including what name is right and staying with it. One must not be afraid to tell others what name is preferred. If it's any consolation, it is more likely that the numbers of transitionals is increasing and the awareness of such problems will be understood.

Many people share their own stories or those of others whose lives illustrate how the cultural images are followed even today, well after the revolution. These stories clearly identify people by their conduct. Of all these stories, Margaret's story provides the best illustration of the old culture images. At the time she told the story she was in her 70's. Her story follows:

> *I first met my husband, David, when we were in college. We got married in our senior year. Both of our parents approved. For me, there never was anyone else. He was all that I could ask for. I know I could have looked around, but I didn't. David was the one, and I think I was the only one for him.*
>
> *Due to the complications with my first pregnancy, I had a miscarriage, and I was told I could never have children. We never did adopt. I know most of my friends have marital problems from time to time, but we didn't. I actually felt sorry for a lot of my friends. I learned that my place was to be silent. I was often embarrassed how perfect our marriage was. In all those years we never had a fight. I know I was lucky, and I had something special. My friends were involved in arguments and disputes with their husbands. I know some even walked out of their marriages and never returned.*
>
> *I didn't work. That's one thing David forbade. He said he was the man of the house and it was his job to take care of me. He did a good job of protecting me, so I didn't argue. Even if I did get a job, I would not have earned much, so it was not worth fighting over. We weren't rich, but we were comfortable, and we were never short of money for the things we really needed.*
>
> *David bought our house at a special price from his father right after we got married. I was a good housewife. I took care of the meals. I did the dishes, the laundry, and cleaned the house. David never complained. He took care of everything else. I heard my friend's stories, but I was convinced that my friends brought their problems on themselves. They seemed to always be challenging their husbands. They wanted a life outside the home, and seemed to be trying to assert their independence. To me, they were asking for trouble when they decided to work. My friends used to say I was too passive, but I didn't have their problems. Besides, David took great pride in providing for me. I lived my life just as I thought all wives should.*
>
> *Then, one day he was gone. He had a fatal heart attack while cutting the lawn. It was totally unexpected. For a long time, I was*

in a state of shock. In all honesty, I was devastated. I can't explain it, really. He was everything to me.

I'm sure he thought he was a good husband, but he left me totally vulnerable, unable to do anything without him. I had never written a check, balanced an account, used a screwdriver, or even changed a light bulb.

Suddenly my total admiration and respect for him and for what he had done for me all those years changed, and I was angry. It wasn't that he died and left me. I learned to accept that. I just couldn't accept the fact he left me totally unprepared for life without him. It wasn't right. I had to borrow money from a friend just to tide me over while his estate was probated. I couldn't help the attorney because I didn't know what David owned, or where he kept things. I had no idea whether he had a lock box or a will.

I find myself hating the man who had done everything for me. I would not wish my fate on anyone. In the end, the man who had cherished and protected me all those years deceived me and left me totally unprepared for life without him.

Margaret and David lived the old culture story. David was the ideal knight in shining armor, and Margaret was the perfect pauper princess. No one could have written a better script for old culture lives. Unfortunately, David remained locked in the old culture images, and never saw Margaret as an equal human being separate from the image of the pauper princess. Unfortunately for Margaret, she also shared that dream.

This inability to see beyond the old culture pictures makes the world appear to be locked in some strange male versus female war. However, before you feel sympathy for Margaret's plight, you must realize that she too was responsible for her predicament. While David lived blindly following the old images, she also lived her life as the dutiful and obedient housewife idealized in the images.

They never fought because Margaret diffused any potential conflict before it could develop by sublimating herself to the old culture story. She saw herself as subservient and obedient in total disregard for her own feelings and desires. She lived as the female merged back into the male with the male the survivor. For all practical purposes, she simply did not exist as a separate individual human being. Unfortunately, she lived a life that mirrors the lives of many old culture females in this country today.

For many transitionals, Margaret's case seems extreme because she never worked, and that, for those a generation younger than her, is rare. The world is changing, but it is only a matter of degree. The old culture bias is still deeply entrenched within us. In the end, Margaret's story tells us why the old culture story of making poor Adam whole again at the expense of the independence of Eve doesn't work. In the fable, everyone lives happily ever after. No one ever dies so old culture men and women do not have to deal with death or reality. In the real world, usually women out live men by several years. The failure of the couple to deal with Adam's death creates an unwarranted hardship for many old culture women.

Margaret's example illustrates two things. First, she lived the life of the classic old culture female well into the Transition. Second, she is also typical of females in the way she assigned blame for her predicament solely on her husband, unaware that the real culprit was culture and that part of the problem was within herself. Margaret's survival now depends on her becoming aware of how the old culture lifestyle trapped them both. Only through forgiveness, not just of David, but of herself will she be ready to survive on her own in the modern world.

Margaret's situation was quite common for her generation, but the world has changed, dragging all of us along with it. The following are Betty's comments, a woman in her mid forties, more than a generation behind Margaret:

> *I feel my life is a vortex of conflicting demands. I am caught between the old standards of my parents and those of a new world my parents never experienced. When I met Ted and we decided to get married, I wanted to work. I had no intentions of simply being a housewife. Ted did not object. He saw the advantage that two incomes allowed us to do a lot of things we otherwise could not afford. We have no children. He makes roughly thirty percent more than I do. We have been married eight years. Ted does help more with the household chores than my father ever did. I think, if we had children, things would have been different. I'm sure I would have had to live a life balancing work and being a mother.*
>
> *I also think we would have had problems if I suddenly got a promotion and started earning more than he did. Being realistic, that would still cause a problem today.*
>
> *At work, I never push. I'm a realist. I'm sure I'll never go any further in the company than where I am now, but I'm content. I like my job. I'm not looking for advancement.*

Betty's world is different from Margaret's, but the old culture is still there. The following comments are Laura's, a young woman under thirty:

> *Stan and I have been living together for over two years. We are not married. The topic has come up, but we are both concentrating on our careers. Stan has a degree in engineering and has worked for the same company since I met him. He seems content with his work. I have a graduate degree, and I changed jobs last year to get the promotion that would keep me on my career track. If I see another company move in a year or two that will advance me toward my goal I'll take it.*
>
> *Right now I'm content. Maybe things will work out where I am, but I have to take advantage of good opportunities when they arise. Stan and I realize we might have to live separately for a while if I get transferred out of town, but for now everything is fine. I make more than Stan, but it doesn't bother him. We both know our salaries and jobs will change from time to time.*
>
> *We have a joint account just for the common expenses. I'm not planning to get pregnant right now, but if I did we would get married. If he left me, I'd still have the baby and bring it up on my own. I'm not sure I'd go out looking for another guy. I'm pretty self-contained. We're together because we want to be. Right now, our careers are the most important thing in our lives.*

The lives of Margaret, Betty, and Laura show how the views and relationships of women have changed over the generations from old culture thinking to transitional. The image of the knight and castle is fading with each passing generation.

There are, however, some people who are locked into the old culture bias, unaware of how its images control their lives. The following are two stories of individuals who, unlike most people, reached a point in life where they no longer had to spend all day trying to earn enough money just to make ends meet. Now they could apply their efforts toward other worthy objectives. Yet, at this important pinnacle where they have the ability to set new standards and provide a positive impact on the world in which they live, they remain unconsciously mired in the old culture, locked in an unsatisfactory, and unrewarding existence.

> *Mary appeared only momentarily on a television show. She was a guest on the show. The hostess was interviewing women who were having trouble finding a husband and were seeking assistance in developing a workable solution to their problem. Mary was introduced as a person of wealth and sophistication. The audience was told she had lost her husband due to a tragedy a couple of years before her appearance on the show. She was somewhere around fifty and confirmed that she had inherited a substantial sum of money from her husband's estate. She explained that she had been on her own since his death, and, while she had made a major effort to find someone, she had only met men interested in her money.*

Of all the men she had met, she concluded none would be supportive and take care of her. She concluded the men were looking for her to take care of them.

The second example is Ed's story:

> *Ed was divorced over three years ago. His ex-wife had been a non-working spouse. Ed was about sixty. In spite of the divorce settlement, he had a substantial nest egg that left him comfortable for life. He claimed his wealth came from the sale of his business. Ed's present interests were his yacht and dating women substantially younger than himself. He said he was anxious to remarry if he could find a suitable wife, but all the young women he met were either too independent or focused on his money. He complained that he could not find that certain someone he was looking for.*

> *There was a woman at the marina where he kept his yacht who was about two years younger than Ed. She had a professional career. Others who knew them both could not understand why Ed saw no interest in this woman instead of the much younger women he spent time with whom he was often seen.*

However, Ed's situation was quite clear. He was strictly old culture. He was looking for a wife who met the old culture image. He was not looking for someone with whom he could share interests. Instead, he was looking for a submissive female who shared his image of what he thought a wife should be. He was looking for a replacement for his first wife, a pauper princess. He had nothing in common with the transitional woman closer to his own age. The women he met now had changed orientation and he had not.

Mary's situation was much the same. She was the one with the wealth, so the old culture images simply did not apply. Unfortunately she was spending her time looking for a knight in shining armor right out of the old culture image. Her problem was that she was the one who owned the castle.

The personal needs of these two people is unknown. They could now live satisfying and rewarding lives free from financial restraints. Yet they remained locked in old culture behavior patterns, unaware of the power the old culture images were forging on their lives. They believed they were seeking goals of happiness and well being. They thought their problems were technique. They were unaware that their problem was one of social orientation.

Another important illustration for this chapter follows:

Tom and Sally were each members of a sailing club. They met at a weekend sailing regatta sponsored by the club. Their small racing sailboats were pulled out of the water at the end of each weekend and stored in the assigned storage bays on shore.

When they married, the club changed their memberships from separate "individual" membership to a joint "family" category. Tom and Sally initially did not object since there was a net savings in dues. However, when Sally was called by the club secretary and told that the club rules allowed only one storage slip per "family," she asked what she should do. Since she and Tom both liked sailing, she was told that the club had a special exception if she gave Tom title to her sailboat so both boats were in his name. Sally objected because she spent her own hard earned money to buy her boat. The club did not yield claiming it was club rules and must be followed. Eventually, Sally moved her sailboat to another club further down the lake.

This example is important for three reasons. First, Tom and Sally are upper income individuals, much like Mary and Ed. Their situation illustrates how the old culture bias can be found at every economic level. Second, when the old culture bias is strongly entrenched, the best practice is avoidance, as illustrated when Sally simply moved her boat to another club on the same lake. Now she and Ted could both sail on the weekends in their own boats. Third, the old culture defies logic or reality. They both had boats, they both were members, they both liked sailing, but the old culture bias residing in the club rules required compliance with its image that married people were one with the female merged into the male. When Tom and Sally married, they moved into the arbitrary family category where husband and wife were merged together as one. The club stood behind the position that now they were one. Again, only the husband survived, right out of the classic story, as evidenced by the special exception for the husband who could have two boats and two slips. This ruling reinforces the belief that the wife simply disappeared on marriage, merged into her husband.

This simple example of how the war is really with culture, not people, and can be found in all aspects of our lives, even on a remote sailing lake. However, the most important aspect of this simple example is how culture puts pressure on property ownership. The club wanted Sally to convey title to her boat over to her husband. There is no such thing as putting your property in someone else's name unless you seek legal help to structure a proper trust relationship. However, even if she and Tom had set up an escrow or trust, it would most likely not have met the requirements of the club, which had clearly expressed itself as old culture. The club was looking for a full transfer and an escrow or trust relationship would most likely have been seen as a subterfuge to try to get around their rules.

On the downside of this example, if Tom and Sally later divorced and title to her boat was in his name, Sally would have faced an up hill struggle to try to establish title to her own sailboat. Sally's battle would become worse if Tom turned hostile, as is usually the case in divorce actions. Avoid getting caught in the trap of yielding to cultural pressure to give up property ownership on the basis of conforming to the concept that married people are one, especially where the net effect is that the male survives and the female disappears. Married people are still separate unique human beings, and they each legally have the right to property ownership that belongs to them individually.

Examples used for upper income people are provided for a reason. The objective is to offset the mistaken belief that the old culture bias resides in those who have little education or income and that social orientation is a function of economic circumstances. For some reason, many people associate old culture thinking with poverty and difficult financial conditions. The reality couldn't be further from the truth. The examples used have been carefully selected to counter that misconception. Old culture thinking exists in anyone in any socioeconomic class. Perhaps the perception is that things are different these days, and the new culture is just around the corner. Review the following enlightening comments:

> *I thought the classification of people as either old culture or transitional was a bit simplistic and consisted of over generalizations. However, last week we went to the shore and I watched young children at play on the beach. The children started out just playing around with their plastic pails and shovels. After a while, the boys settled down either individually or in groups of two or three, busily started building castles in the sand with moats and towers. After a few minutes, the little girls joined them. They struggled together totally aware that the rising tide was going to destroy their castles, but they remained resolute in their effort to build them.*

Frankly, the observation was a bit chilling. None of them built a Santa Clause, an Easter Bunny, or anything else for that matter. All I saw were castles in the sand. The old culture images were there in these young children and they would stay with them for the rest of their lives. Even at their young ages, the cultural images were already deeply planted in their minds.

Old culture thinking influences both the ownership of property and personal relationships in many ways. The key to survival today is to learn to be aware of how old customs, traditions, and biases result in behavior and thought patterns that can potentially restrict one's life unconsciously. The prescription for prevention is to develop a level of awareness that will allow detection of the adverse effect that this bias may cause before the damage is done or the trap is constructed and affects one personally and/or financially.

CHAPTER FIFTEEN: LIGHT AT THE END OF THE TUNNEL

One of the common criticisms of the different estates in property ownership is that it is a waste of time because property is in the hands of men, not women. The bias against women keeps females suppressed because control of wealth is seen as synonymous with the control of power. To those critics, women are trapped in a dark tunnel with no hope in sight, constrained to second-class citizenship. These critics often claim that promoting the premise that the struggle is against culture and not men does no good as long as men maintain control of property. For the same reason, such critics see teaching women increased awareness of property rights serves no valuable purpose.

Thankfully, there is a light at the end of the tunnel of darkness. In fact, it is easy to understand that some of the critics are overwhelmed. Clearly, an excessive barrage of anti-female rhetoric has prevailed in this country since the beginning of the revolution. Occasionally, things may appear a bit bleak. On the other hand, there is no basis for such pessimism.

Our forefathers came to this country to escape a political system based on privilege, not on equality and the value of the individual. The English system is based on the arbitrary concept of privilege by sex and birth order. Back across the ocean, people even selected their leaders, not by skill or ability, but solely by blood relationships. The entire system of property rights was based on legal devices structured to keep wealth in the hands of the privileged few, determined by gender and birth order.

The first settlers of this country came from the disenfranchised and not the landed aristocracy. The old English system was repugnant to them. They wanted something new. They wanted a chance to better themselves during their lifetime. As a result, the settlers of this country rejected the old system of special privilege as a means to control property ownership. The critics have overlooked this rejection of a system based on privilege by birthright and how it affects women in favorable ways. This change in how property may be acquired produces that light at the end of the tunnel.

To understand how this happens, review of the joint tenancy between married persons and the joint tenancy with rights of survivorship provides a place to begin. Both of these estates carry with them the condition of survivorship. One or the other of these estates is used in virtually all real estate transactions by married couples in this country today. Forget for the moment whether use of this estate is a good practice in all cases. The use of the survivorship element is a practical reality, done automatically, without consideration for the source of the financial contribution of the respective spouses.

Back in the American Dark Ages, males controlled income as well as financial wealth. Yet, starting back then, the custom that continues to this day is for married couples to purchase their homes using the survivorship estate. To accept or reject the premise as to why this happens, recognize that the survivorship element dominates real estate transactions where married couples are the buyers. The preference for this gender-neutral survivorship estate is responsible for the light at the end of the tunnel.

There is another factor in favor of women, when combined with survivorship, allows the light to burn brighter. The combination of survivorship and this additional factor has the effect of moving property from husbands and males over to wives and other females, thus shifting economic power base from men over to women. For better or worse, the power of this reverse bias lies with the grim reaper. Statistics, no matter where published, all demonstrate the same fact that, as a general rule, women outlive men. Whether the study shows a life span difference at five years or fifteen years, no study shows men statistically outliving women. Going one step further, if both spouses are born on the same date, or on an average, the husband is older than his wife by several years; the female statistically outlives her spouse. Every marriage where an older male marries a younger female, the figures are distorted even more dramatically in favor of the female. The truth is that, statistically, wives outlive their husbands by a significant number of years.

This fact may make the old culture male feel a bit uneasy, but the reality is that jointly held real estate with the survivorship element will ultimately be owned by the wife alone. This fact becomes important recognizing that for the average married couple their wealth is primarily in the equity in their home. The net affect is that personal wealth in this country is shifting from men over to women. In fact, this change is taking place at such a rapid rate that sometime in the next few years, depending again on which figures are used, women will own the majority of the wealth in this country. As a corollary, since wealth is power, there is truly a light at the end of the tunnel for women. For valid reasons, women need to focus their attention on increasing knowledge and awareness of property rights and the influence of cultural bias on property ownership.

However, there is one ownership situation that keeps the flame from growing bright. The dangerous situation exists where the woman moves into the castle owned solely by the knight, especially if she has small children from a prior marriage. Under these conditions, the castle remains owned by the knight and the wife really becomes the pauper princess. If he dies first, the castle does not automatically become hers, and her right to continue to occupy the home will depend on state law. The problem, of course, resides in the laws relating to the rights of non-owner spouses, which vary significantly from state to state. Because the house was in his name only, it will be an asset in his estate on his death. If he dies without a will state intestate laws will determine who receives his net estate after all costs are paid.

State inheritance laws usually give a large share of a husband's estate to his spouse, however, title to the house itself depends on the degree to which the estate is solvent. If the estate does not have enough cash to pay all costs and expenses, the property may have to be sold to pay outstanding obligations. In such cases, the spouse will only receive her statutory share of the net estate after the home is sold. Because real estate is the one asset that builds equity over time, the failure to obtain the castle through the knight's estate can cause the light in the tunnel to flicker.

If the knight dies leaving a will, the issue of solvency again determines what assets are left when the will is applied. If the estate is solvent and the castle survives the solvency test, it could be the subject of a specific bequest to someone other than the surviving spouse. In most states a spouse does have a right to elect a specific share of the estate if she is not satisfied with what she would receive under the will. The danger is that these provisions usually do not provide for a specific right to specific property and, once again, the castle can be lost. The only other hope for the spouse is to thoroughly analyze any state rights that may exist because the castle was the family home. In some states, the right of a non-owner spouse can become vested ownership rights after a set period of time, so state law must be reviewed carefully.

Even if the knight executes a will leaving the castle to his wife or her children as an inducement for her to move in, he can change the will at any time. This inducement then offers no security to the non-owner spouse.

Most possessory rights of a spouse in the castle owned solely by the knight are not sufficient to provide fuel to the flickering flame in the tunnel, and the knight's invitation to just move in remains a dangerous situation especially for the woman who has children from a prior marriage. Every woman instinctively wants to protect her children while alive and works to maximize what she can do for her children to protect them when she is gone. The home as the castle in the old culture image is the one asset that is most likely to increase in value over time. The natural goal of every mother is to give her children a real interest in the castle if she can. For this reason, the invitation to move into the castle owned solely by a new spouse is often a dangerous situation for the woman with children from a previous relationship.

The most dangerous situation for the women with children from a previous relationship is the one where she moves in, does not have any ownership rights, and she dies first. In most states, her children will have no interest in the castle owned by her second spouse. Even if he adopts her children or provides for them in a will, the property owned in his name only remains his on her death and he can do what he wants with it during his lifetime. The key of course is that on her death, the house is still owned by the knight. There are some states that have community property statues or laws that turn the rights of the non-owner spouse into true ownership often after some required occupancy period as spouse. Even in these cases there are dangers if the couple moves from one house to another, especially if the move involves relocating from one state to another.

The woman with children from a prior relationship who moves into the castle owned solely by the knight must be alert for the promise by the knight to take care of her and her children. She must insist that his intentions be prepared in writing in a will where such promise is used as an inducement for her to move into the castle. This is important where the legal relationship of marriage is not a part of the promise. A will is not a legally binding document until the one who signs it dies and the will is probated without challenge. During the lifetime of the one signing the will, the will may be amended in almost any way by codicil or even completely revoked at any time. As such, a will offers no security for any named beneficiary or devisee. Most rights of a spouse in the castle owned of record solely by the knight are not sufficient to provide fuel to the flickering flame in the tunnel. The knight's invitation to just move in is dangerous for the woman who has children from a prior relationship. The children are not protected if she dies.

Even though the use of the survivorship estate is transferring the wealth of the country from men to women, it still may not be the right estate to use in light of specific individual circumstances. If the knight survives his spouse, the property is then owned solely by him and once again her children have no interest in the property. Where the knight owns the castle in his name only, the only way her children will obtain an interest in the castle after her death include the following:

    a. The surviving spouse deeds them an interest as a gift.
    b. The surviving spouse sells them an interest for consideration.
    c. The surviving spouse adopts them and then dies intestate.
    d. The surviving spouse executes a will and devises them an interest in the property.

Simply stated, whether one dies testate with a will or intestate without a will, ownership in property as joint tenants with rights of survivorship with a second spouse does not allow an interest in the property into your asset estate at death. Children will again have no interest in the castle. The following comment provides an example of a woman who shows an awareness of the danger:

> *I'll marry you as long as we can protect my kids in case something happens to me. I think we need to see a lawyer and work things out. I'm worried about the consequences of simply moving into your house.*

The above response indicates awareness, not of the answers, but of a need to ask questions and find the answers before she steps into a new marriage or relationship. The key for women is to be aware of the issues, and to realize that what happens ultimately depends on the answers to the questions. Also crucial, is the need to be aware that if one does not speak up and make desires known, others will make assumptions that may not be in one's best interests. Increased awareness is part of the fuel that keeps the fire burning at the end of the tunnel.

Our forefathers originally came from a land where the key element to the wealth of their property depended not on equality or merit or but on laws that gave special privilege to the first-born male. This is the system and concept our forefathers sought to escape when they came to this country. The concept of privilege has no place in our state laws. Instead, levels of relationships within categories are given equal weight. For example, if parents survive the death of a child, the parents inherit equally regardless of sex. This concept is carried over to the category of children.

If three children survive the death of their parents, they inherit equally among them as children. Each receives an undivided one-third interest as tenants in common. The sex, birth order, and age of the children have no impact on our inheritance laws. This fact is not emphasized in the media because it does not fit the old culture images. The fact that our laws are neutral as to gender provides the reason for the light at the end of the tunnel.

Of course, the response of the critics is that our inheritance laws apply if you die without a will. There are no laws against bias in the preparation of a will, so the parent who wishes to assert a male or female bias in a will can legally do so. While it is true there are no rules prohibiting gender bias in the preparation of wills, our society has not adopted a general bias in favor of first born males even when preparing a will. As a general observation, people in this country think in terms of children. However, the bias factor historically has crept into the wills of parents who own commercial and business property where they have shown some bias in favor of male children. However, this bias is often more a concern about the lack of interest or capacity of female children to manage commercial property than it is an adoption of old concepts from across the ocean.

Business assets will be handled more equally as daughters become more transitional and escape the old culture in their acts and interests. As fathers watch their daughters obtain an education in business and finance or select professional careers, this old culture bias is likely to yield to the modern reality of equality between children even in the preparation of wills.

Of course, part of the solution means mothers must tell their daughters the truth that the old childhood story of the knights in shining armor and the pauper princess are fables, or myths like the other stories of their childhood. When their daughters reject the old culture and refuse to wait for their knight to show up, the significant males in their lives will see them as equal to their brothers in the ability to manage commercial business assets, and equal treatment between children will follow.

In conclusion, the light at the end of the tunnel is real simply because there is no anti-female bias in our property laws, including laws that regulate the distribution of property on the death of the owner. In fact, the one place where the image of the old culture bias comes through is the selection of survivorship estates as the way married people own property. This type of ownership results in the steady transfer of property over to women. Ultimately, women will soon own the majority of the wealth in this country. Once women have total dominion and control of property, they can then be sure it is distributed to their children.

The pessimists who see only a struggle of controlling men dominating second-class women may be surprised to know that the transfer of wealth to women is underway. Men are facilitating the transfer by following the old culture custom of conveying property into survivorship estates. However, the bleak view of the pessimists can still become a reality. If old culture women willingly give their property to their husbands on marriage, men would own all property and the light in the tunnel is threatened. Only awareness that every financial transaction involves a need to ask questions and identify the old culture dangers in the transaction can keep the flame alive. The light at the end of the tunnel will do women no good if the power of culture prevents women from becoming aware the light is there.

In the meantime, instead of waiting for the shift in wealth to take place, women must focus on reality and increasing their knowledge and awareness of the dangers and pitfalls that lurk in every property transaction. Without enlightened vigilance, the light at the end of the tunnel can flicker and go out.

CHAPTER SIXTEEN: A REALITY CHECK

Love can be dangerous to one's personal and financial good health.

The danger of love is often expressed in the phrase, "love is blind" or that people are blind about love. All anyone knows for sure is that there is a powerful sexual attraction between men and women that happens spontaneously, beyond their control. This event happens with one out of every so many hundred people of the opposite sex. Beyond that, we know very little more about it, except that it is blind, just as the phrase states. Love does not differentiate rich from poor, good from bad, even young from old. In fact, love is blind as to race, creed, color, or national origin. Moreover, the matching power of love is blind to social orientation and does not differentiate old culture people from transitionals.

Whenever love occurs, there is almost always some form of self-deception and denial about the relationship that comes with it. The emotion felt is so positive and uplifting that those "in love" will do almost anything to maintain and nurture the feeling. The one "in love" often rejects anything that could possibly threaten this feeling of euphoria. For this reason, some people compare the feeling of love to a drug. There is a strong similarity in the desire to prolong this positive chemical reaction in the brain. In fact, the one in love finds this feeling so pleasant, they often ignore common sense altogether and undertake acts that are not always in their best interests. The danger of love is so strong that it can blot out all aspects of reality.

The danger is that love may block out conflicting social orientations in the force to cultivate and reinforce the love relationship. Too often this process takes place unconsciously, trapping even rational or transitional people. How often has an old culture female said:

> *Don't tell me anything negative about him. I don't want to hear it. I don't want to know.*

In fact, to even suggest to the one in love that their newfound love interest is less than perfect is to risk the friendship. Many best friends have lost a relationship over even a casual comment if the one in love sees the remark as a criticism. No one wants to hear any negative advice about their love interest no matter how well intended or accurate it may be. This natural reaction is most extreme when it comes to love.

As a result, friends, parents, business associates, and relatives are often inclined not to comment about what they see in a person's love interest. Instead, they will keep quiet and maintain the relationship and not discuss the love interest honestly. Yet, in many ways, this is the time when a good, honest advice is often needed. When a person is "in love," it is the one time a heavy injection of reality is needed. In reality, marriage is a legal relationship, involving property rights and living with someone on a day-to-day basis. This pitfall can result in the harshest of realities when feelings turn bad and former lovers retaliate for perceived wrongs.

Every practicing attorney specializing in matrimonial cases has a file storage facility bursting at the seams with files of failed marriages and bitter battles. To imagine the heartache and trauma that those files represent is difficult, but they indicate two things about love. First, this feeling of love often wears off after a period of time if it is not nurtured mutually. Secondly, the parties in those failed marriages started out "in love." Living with another person requires the partners think alike, have compatible perceptions or are willing to communicate effectively, compromise and respect the other's opinions and perceptions. Generally, this means that the parties have the same social orientation. The message inherent in the warehouse of divorce files is that transitional people and old culture people do not mix and cannot live together. If married partners find themselves in love, the euphoria will not overcome the reality clashes of different social orientations.

How many parents feel the man their daughter has selected, or visa versa, is not worthy of her/his interest? How often is this opinion nothing more than the expression that the mate selected does not meet the parent's old culture image of the knight in shining armor or pauper princess? Is their real objection that the knight has bought the armor with his bank charge card, and is making monthly payments for the mighty steed that will not be paid for until it is ready to be retired? Are they concerned because the blissful couple will have to rent an apartment in the village until they can save enough money for a down payment on the castle? Are they concerned about her happiness, or the preservation of their personal old culture images?

Sometimes the situation is reversed and the parents are anxiously pushing the daughter into marriage in spite of the daughter's reservations. Old culture parents, who reach the stage where they approve of the knight, will often do whatever they can to make poor Adam whole again by minimizing their daughter's concerns. A middle-aged woman said it best:

> *I was young and was swept up in all the details of planning for the wedding. When I had doubts at the last minute, I felt guilty. My parents were spending a large part of their savings on my wedding, so I didn't say anything. At the time, I didn't want to disappoint them. Looking back now, what I really did was ruin my life. Now it's too late for me. I lived my life to make others happy. I never lived for myself.*

Do parents ever feel any guilt they helped create the picture their daughter internalizes and finally acts out? Of course, the parents, too, were victims. The images they passed on to their daughter were really the culture of their generation, and that was during a time when the images were much closer to reality than they are today. A transitional woman shows a different approach to love:

> *I love him dearly, but I won't marry him. I'll spend time with him, but I can't live with him.*

She recognizes that love and marriage are not the same thing. Love is an emotional state. Marriage, on the other hand, is a legal relationship and many factors are involved in determining its success. However, many people still lump love and marriage together and feel the emotional state is something so special it must be accepted blindly and memorialized by marriage. The following comment is not that unusual:

> *I don't feel comfortable discussing these matters. Love is something that should be accepted without question. People who are in love should get married.*

The fact that she feels uncomfortable means she is in conflict with the old culture images within herself. The social revolution has changed the world forever. The topic of love and marriage may still be an uncomfortable topic for some who are old culture. Today, the analysis of love and marriage is extremely relevant if those "in love" avoid the warehouse of failed marriages. Marriage candidates need to have a clear understanding of what marriage means to them. The concept that people "in love" should get married is evidence of the old culture attitude. This attitude is dangerous and out of date. She clings to old culture thinking because it gives her a feeling of security and security is the lure of the old culture. The following example demonstrates of why the old attitudes towards marriage are now a danger:

> *I need a good lawyer. I want a divorce and I want to sue this man for fraud. The ring he gave me is real but the diamond is not what I was expecting. The house is beautiful, but it is rented on a month-to-month basis, just like his expensive car. His fancy looking watch is a knock-off.*

Obviously, poor Adam was willing to go to any length to desperately entice his pauper princess into making himself whole again. Apparently, he may have strayed a bit beyond normal bounds of an acceptable courtship. Her reaction is more interesting. She appears to be saying she is willing to go to court and testify that she is old culture and she is entitled to rely on the male to support her. To her, his failure to provide her with expected old culture rewards for having married him is not only the basis for divorce, but also grounds for damages on the basis of fraud. Is the ring just a symbol of the relationship where its economic value is of no significance, or is its economic value a key element of the marriage itself? Strikingly, her comment indicates the relationship between the parties is of no importance because she doesn't even mention it. Clearly, he did not live up to her expectations of what marriage means to her. Apparently, ownership of the castle and the trusty steed by the knight, to her, are important prerequisites for a successful marriage.

Awareness means taking into account that marriage means different things to different people. Burying one's head in the sand and denying the fact that people are unique individuals is not a realistic approach in the world today. The following woman's comment reveals she is finally becoming aware of the influence of the old culture on her life:

> *The last time I was in love, I closed my eyes. I wound up divorced supporting a small child on my own. Next time, if there is one, I'm going to keep my eyes wide open even for that first kiss.*

Once aware that love is blind, the right attitude is to seek advice from others to offset the inability to see clearly. While caution is commendable, danger still lurks in decision-making. People sought for advise are likely to be wary of being honest at the risk of the relationship, even when sincerely asked. Reassuring them that honest criticism is welcomed and desired, and they will not jeopardize the relationship or be penalized for their comments. They will be of no assistance. In fact, actions and words may already have prejudiced their opinions and advice. The second danger is that one must always be suspicious of any advice requested, whether volunteered or solicited, because others frequently may have a hidden agenda behind their comments. For example, those who have miserable marriages frequently do not want others to have happy and fulfilling relationships. These people will sometimes provide harmful advice to undermine a good relationship so that others will suffer the same as they do.

More seriously, the social orientation of the advisers often plays a large role in the advice they provide. An adviser may pressure others into marriage basically to reaffirm their own old culture orientation. They may simply have a strong desire to make poor Adam whole again. Once aware of one's old culture orientation, responses to questions may be predictable, even before the question is asked.

Always remember that old culture people are very predictable. Frequently, old culture people are totally unaware of the basis for their own actions or opinions. When talking to old culture relatives, don't be too quick to blame them for who they are. Only a truly transitional person may provide a fair and unbiased opinion about love and marriage. The following old culture responses tell what marriage means to them. Be on guard if any of these responses surface:

> *Don't worry about anything. Everyone gets cold feet. Everything will work out just fine.*

> *Relax and give yourself some time. You can change him after you're married.*

> *There is only one true love in life. Once you find that special person, you have to accept the good with the bad.*

> *Give your marriage a chance. Everything takes time.*

> *Try to work things out. I did and I've been married for 20 years.*

> *The invitations are all in the mail. I can't stop it now. What will people say?*
>
> *A woman's role is to back up her husband. You have to yield to your husband's desires to make things work.*

Old culture people will use the above responses no matter what question is asked. Their responses will always be aimed at encouraging others to marry because they need to reaffirm their internal images of the cultural myth. Remember, personal feelings are insignificant in the need to make poor Adam whole again. Those who do not get married cannot celebrate the merger of the female back into the male, the core element of the old fable images. For these people, once married all problems will simply go away. In the old culture marriage, the female simply disappears, taking her questions with her. Be alert to the responses of the old culture person, no matter what the relationship is. Their responses will always be tainted by their old culture attitudes, especially in relationship to love and marriage.

There is another danger to be aware of in relation to love. Everyone faces loneliness from time to time, but for many people it becomes obsessive. Certainly, the old culture person who believes marriage is the merger of the partners together as one sees marriage as the built-in solution to loneliness. From their perspective, the partners are bound together as one. Old culture people don't like to be alone, even for a minute. Generally, they have a deep-seated need to be near other people all the time.

Transitional people are far more independent and are in control of their emotions, including feelings of loneliness. For transitionals, the initial danger is that old culture people are often inclined to enter into and maintain a marriage simply to avoid loneliness. We have heard in popular songs that "people who need people are the happiest people in the world," and are well adjusted. The danger lies in the fear of loneliness that grows to the extent that one will do virtually anything to develop relationships, regardless of the personal consequences. Police officers fear the call for aid in a domestic crisis, as this call is the most dangerous situation to respond to. Frequently, the spouse who makes the call, seeking aid, turns on the helpers if they feel they will lose the attention of the other spouse for any period of time.

Often the irrational fear of loneliness motivates an abused spouse to return to the abusive relationship, over and over again. The fear of loneliness is a factor in the need for love and is one of the reasons that finding the right answers to personal questions regarding love is so difficult. Many people remain in abusive relationships because they fear the unknown. They are more comfortable with the abuse they know than to face the challenge of an unknown future and possible loneliness.

The professional career woman who has sacrificed a personal life to advance her career is often an easy mark for the old culture media that stresses that time is running out for her to have a family. The old culture bias in her psyche can push her subconsciously to think that she needs to find a husband. If she is truly transitional, such attempts to stir up panic will not work. Looking for a husband is purely old culture, and her efforts will attract only old culture males, exactly what a transitional female does not need. She must find someone with common interests. Developing the right relationship is the goal, not the old stereotyped concept of marriage.

Always remember that the old culture male lurks in the background looking for a way to make poor Adam whole again. The moment a female walks into a sports bar or nightclub in search of a husband, the old culture male will be at her side offering to buy her a drink. In his need to make poor Adam whole again, his picture of a wife remains cemented in the old culture images no matter how charming he may appear when she meets him.

To avoid the trap of settling on an old culture male, the transitional woman must have a clear perception of who she is and what marriage means to her. Stereotyped role-playing is the cornerstone of the old culture concept of marriage, as is the process of courtship. This means one must be alert when meeting potential love partners. No matter how charming and wonderful an old culture person may appear, they will consciously avoid entering into meaningful communication on any real issue, deliberately diverting any effort to discover their old culture attitude, right up to and through the marriage. No matter how great the desire to find the right relationship in life, never be deluded that a transitional person can live within the narrow confines of acceptable behavior required and demanded by the old culture male. Many apparently transitional women have convinced themselves that they could successfully settle for an old culture male and adjust to his old culture ways. These failed attempts at such compromised relationships fill the storage files of divorce attorneys.

Once one's attitude becomes transitional, one can never go back to being old culture in orientation. The effects of the revolution are permanent, just as is the change in social orientation from old culture to transitional. Developing the awareness that loneliness is a factor in everyone's life and the desire to find the ideal partner are common issues for everyone. This awareness demands acceptance for achieving a happy, successful life. The successful individual deals with the downside of these issues by developing a few outside interests to challenge the mind and abilities. The danger is not in the goals, but in the compromises made to achieve these goals.

Because love can be blind and people, whether old culture or transitional, can be blind about love, the checklist in this chapter provides a tool to identify some of the issues to be addressed prior to marriage. The checklist is structured to create direct communication between love partners. Potential marriage partners often ignore the issues in their relationship due to the emotional euphoria of being "in love." This euphoria may override the need to determine whether the partners truly have compatible social orientations. This failure to deal with reality will have a significant impact on whether the newfound love relationship winds up in the ever expanding warehouse of failed marriages or succeeds.

If the goal is to turn the emotion of love into a long-term relationship, replacement of the old stereotyped images of love with a true interest in the individual is critical. The application of common sense and real assessment of social orientation of both partners, specific circumstances, and financial assets plays a major role in determining the person selected to build a permanent relationship.

Making firm rules about love is difficult. Without that magic spark that is so essential for creating the euphoria, any relationship has the potential never to get off the ground. The best practice for success is to balance practicality against emotional needs and use the knowledge of social orientations to avoid the dangers facing each important life issue.

The checklist consists of two parts. The first section provides hypothetical sketches followed by a number of statements addressing the issues raised by the sketch. The second part of the checklist provides short statements. To use the checklist effectively, make two copies, giving one copy to each of the partners. Each person is to complete their checklist in private so neither one influences the other's personal responses and to ensure honesty. The checklist is simple to complete. Simply mark an "X" in either the "yes" or the "no" column opposite each statement.

The objective of this exercise is to address issues marriage partners are likely to face during their life together to determine if the parties are compatible. The goal is to address these issues as hypothetical, before they appear in the context of a more complex and emotionally charged real-life situations. Many divorce files indicate that marriages often fail due to issues that could have been addressed before the marriage, but were ignored. After time, the solutions were difficult because the legal relationship of marriage altered the perspective of the participants and the expectations of the partners were never honestly evaluated.

Awareness of the need to define what marriage means to each individual is the key to building a strong foundation for a lasting relationship. Hopefully, the effort spent on this checklist will replace the focus on the details of the marriage ceremony that distract the parties from addressing the real issues.

REALITY CHECKLIST

First Hypothetical Case

James and Janice plan to get married. They are both in their early twenties and are each considering marriage for the first time. They each have only a few hundred dollars in their separate checking accounts. They plan to live in an apartment. Only James is employed at the time of their marriage.

Statement	Response	Yes	No

Statement 01

Once they are married, they should open a joint checking account and close their separate accounts. ____ ____

Statement 02

They should keep their existing separate accounts and open a new, joint account just for common expenses as rent and food. ____ ____

Statement 03

They should open a new joint account because they are married, but James should write all the checks because he is the only one producing an income. ____ ____

Statement 04

They should open a new joint account since they are married. Janice should handle the money and write all the checks to take the pressure off James, allowing him to focus on his job. ____ ____

Statement 05

Since James is the only one earning an income, he should be the one to set the budget for all personal expenses. ____ ____

Statement	Response	Yes	No

Statement 06

Since Janice has the time, she should pay all the bills out of their new, joint account and create personal budgets for their personal expenses.   ____ ____

Statement 07

The money in their personal checking accounts accumulated before the marriage should remain in their individual names.   ____ ____

Statement 08

All finances should be handled by joint decisions regardless of who works. All money earned during the marriage belongs to both of them.   ____ ____

Second Hypothetical Case

The facts provided in the first hypothetical case remain the same, except after they are married, Janice obtains a job that pays roughly the same as James.

Statement 01

If they had separate checking accounts before she was employed, they should continue to maintain separate accounts keeping separate records. They can alternate months as to who pays the common expenses.   ____ ____

Statement 02

If they had separate accounts, they should now combine them. As married persons, they should now operate as one since they are both employed.   ____ ____

| Statement | Response | Yes | No |

Statement 03

Since they are both working, they should have only one account with both having individual signature power. All personal funds should now be transferred into this one account. All decisions should be made together. ____ ____

Statement 04

They should have one joint account for common expenses. Each should contribute an equal agreed upon amount to this account each month. The rest of their income is their own individually. ____ ____

Statement 05

As husband, James should continue to handle all the finances regardless of their individual incomes. ____ ____

Third Hypothetical Case

In the first and second hypothetical cases, a year after their marriage Janice inherits the sum of $100,000.00.

Statement 01

All funds accumulated by either party after marriage belong to them jointly because they are married. Her inheritance should be put in one account in both names. ____ ____

Statement 02

Just because people are married to each other does not mean everything belongs to them together. They should keep individual property separately from each other. ____ ____

| Statement | Response | Yes | No |

Statement 03

The funds should be turned over to James since he is the husband and is responsible for all financial matters. ____ ____

Statement 04

The funds should be split in two with each putting half in individual accounts since they are separate people. ____ ____

Fourth Hypothetical Case

Everything is the same at the above hypothetical case except James inherits $100,000 instead of Janice.

Statement 01

It makes no difference who inherits the money. It belongs to both because it was received after they were married. ____ ____

Statement 02

Marriage is an emotional relationship between two people. It has nothing to do with their separate property. ____ ____

Statement 03

Financial assets should always be owned and controlled by the husband regardless of their source. ____ ____

Statement 04

The person who receives financial assets must decide if they want to contribute assets to the other spouse. This must be an individual decision. ____ ____

| Statement | Response | Yes | No |

Fifth Hypothetical Case

Harry has a daughter from a previous marriage. Harriet has two children from her first marriage. Harry tells Harriet they can live in his home since it is paid for. In the state where the property is located, a non-owner spouse has a right to live in the property of the owner spouse as long as they are married.

Statement 01

Harriet should not marry Harry unless he transfers title to
the property into both names as tenants in common to
protect her children in case something happens to her.   ____   ____

Statement 02

Harriet should not complain since the home costs her nothing.
She should accept what he offers and ask for no more. Harry is
obligated to provide a home for his family.   ____   ____

Statement 03

If Harriet says nothing about the house and goes through
with the marriage, she has no right to ask Harry to change
the deed at a later date.   ____   ____

Sixth Hypothetical Case

Sam has an account at a department store in his own name and has a credit card in his name to access the account. Because he has been a good customer for years, he has a high credit limit. His wife, Sally, has an account in her maiden name, but her account credit limit is low.

Statement 01

Because Sam's account has the higher limit, Sally should
close her account. They can apply for a separate credit card
issued to Sally out of his account.   ____   ____

| Statement | Response | Yes | No |

Statement 02

Sally should keep her own account so she can build and
maintain her own credit rating.   ____ ____

Seventh Hypothetical Case

Michelle and Stan have been living together for two years. They are both employed and share common expenses, but they are not married. Using her own funds, Michelle enters and wins the state million-dollar jackpot lottery.

Statement 01

The funds are hers alone because they are not legally
married.   ____ ____

Statement 02

The funds should be shared since they are partners.   ____ ____

Statement 03

Whether they are married or not, she should not tell Stan
about the winnings to save the relationship.   ____ ____

Statement 04

If they married and she did not work and she purchased the
lottery ticket from her allowance, the funds would belong to
both because he earned the money used to buy
the ticket.   ____ ____

Part 2: General Statements

| Statement | Response | Yes | No |

01. Women are unfairly stereotyped by men.   ____ ____

Statement	Response	Yes	No

02. Men are unfairly stereotyped by women.

03. Men are more deeply affected by divorce than women.

04. If the husband makes enough money to support his family, his wife should not work

05. A woman cannot both take care of her home and have an executive position at the same time.

06. A child between the ages of 4 to 6 is better off in day-care so he/she can meet teachers and interact with children of the same age rather than staying home with the mother.

06. Families should be limited to one child because of world population growth.

08. If one partner believes that sex is only for having babies, this fact should be shared before marriage.

09. The insistence on having biological children is selfish. Couples should consider adoption first to take care of children without parents.

10. Sexual needs and expectations are too emotionally charged issues to discuss before marriage.

11. The maximum number of children in any family should not exceed three.

12. Either or both parents may have to move into the marital home. Married partners need to plan for this possibility.

13. Marriages should never break up over such things as a particular brand of household or personal product.

14. If the husband insists on a specific brand of toothpaste or bathing soap, the wife should use the same brand.

| Statement | Response | Yes | No |

15. If a spouse's preferences differ on household products, they should simply buy their preferred brand and not share. Men and women are separate individuals. They do not need to share everything as one. ____ ____

16. If the husband and wife come from different ethnic and/or religious backgrounds, their children should be brought up under the background of the husband. ____ ____

17. Children whose parents are of mixed ethnic/religious backgrounds should be allowed to make their own choices, when old enough to understand the differences. ____ ____

18. If one spouse owns a home in their own name before marriage and the couple plan to live in the house after marriage, the house should be titled in both names. ____ ____

19. If a married couple buys any substantial personal property, title should be in both names because they are married. ____ ____

20. Married couples should file joint tax returns because they are married. ____ ____

21. A woman should change her name on all her identification and assets to her new married name after the wedding. ____ ____

22. Visits to the husband's relatives should always have priority over those of the wife's relatives. ____ ____

23. The husband should decide timing and destination of vacations. ____ ____

24. If both spouses work and earn the same amount of money, the phone listing should still be in the name of the husband because he is head of the household. ____ ____

| Statement | Response | Yes | No |

25. The fact that a woman executive's income exceeds her husband's income will ultimately damage or destroy the marriage. ____ ____

26. If the husband uses a nickname for his wife such as Bambi, Kitten, Cupcake, or Sugar, she should live with it and say nothing because nicknames are harmless. ____ ____

27. The mother, not the father, should give the bride away in the marriage ceremony. ____ ____

28. Bill plays poker with his buddies on Friday nights. He should only play when his wife Janice goes to the movies with her friends. ____ ____

29. Bill and Janice are married. They should take all of their vacations together. ____ ____

30. Since Bill makes more money than Janice, he should make the final decisions about where they go on vacation and how much money they should spend. ____ ____

The above statements are certainly not the only ones that could be used in the checklist. They don't address many other issues involved in a marriage relationship. The topics included are representative of issues that have caused problems or trouble for many relationships. They are presented to provide a useful tool for a pre-marital checklist. Prior to marriage, each partner in the relationship may add additional personal issues to the checklist that are known to be specific to the relationship. For successful relationships, the partners need to discuss the issues openly and honestly.

After completing the responses on the checklist and comparing them with the responses from the prospective partner, the parties will be faced with one of two possible outcomes. Either the responses are substantially the same or they are significantly different. The real objective of the checklist is to draw out the social orientation of the individuals so that each may be aware of the opinions and attitudes of the other before the wedding or cohabitation. If one of the individuals hold tenaciously to an old culture bias and differs from the other who is in transition, the result could indicate where the relationship is destined. If the parties agree on the issues, they are on track to developing a workable relationship.

If there are substantial differences between the responses, one may be old culture in orientation and the other transitional. As a general observation in this situation, a danger sign has just been raised for the couple. The two orientations don't mix well and serious conflicts are likely to result if the relationship continues. Avoidance is the only solution when social orientations clash.

If the results are so similar the differences appear minor, don't throw the checklist away and rush off to a good dinner in a fancy restaurant to celebrate. Instead, carefully review the specific items where there are differences. Many divorce cases reveal that what appeared to be a minor difference over an issue grew seemingly out of proportion, eventually destroying the relationship. Thus, go to dinner, but bring the responses and discuss the specific items where they exist in a relaxed atmosphere. Sometimes the differences over minor items are a matter of personal preferences that can be solved with a reasonable compromise.

However, some people will go to great lengths to preserve a relationship by disguising their true feelings and beliefs. These people occasionally attempt to guess what the other person expects of them and acts accordingly. The only evidence of this subterfuge may be a few key items where true feelings are not disclosed but some minor disagreement is detected. In talking through the specific issues, expand the conversation watching for additional evidence of an attempt to hide a deeper differing orientation.

Naturally, people are tempted to compromise on what appears to be a minor matter for the sake of the relationship. Rather than causing discomfort or disagreement, people often sidestep minor differences because it is easier. The ultimate question is whether what appears to be a small difference is actually an indication of a deeper impasse, not just a passing whim. Often a matter of personal preference can be worked out, but be careful when it is not.

For responses that are substantially different or vary between the respondents, identify what the key issues are before scheduling a candlelight dinner. Take the time to review the exact issues where the differences exist. In any relationship, respect for those differences will eliminate any pressure to buckle under to the other's opinions. The more pressure to compromise, the more likely there is a case of the old culture orientation attempting to dominate a transitional person, trapping the individual in an unacceptable bind. Each partner needs to know in advance where acceptable compromise exists and where to draw the line for their own personal comfort. The ultimate meeting for discussion is probably better in a more private location than a restaurant. Facing a serious impasse may be somewhat awkward and painful, but it is better to know sooner than later. Frequently in marriages, after 12 to 24 months, many women admit to identifying the first signs of major problems and conflicts.

Be wary of the tendency of others to appear to compromise to hold the relationship together. Women who claim that they did not see the warning signs up front may have been duped, but they may have seen the issues and unconsciously or deliberately blocked or avoided addressing them. Other women simply assume they could change their prospective spouse later. Individual cultural orientation is strong and resistant to change. Never be deluded into believing that changing the social and cultural orientation of another person is possible, particularly an old culture orientation.

Only if mutually acceptable compromises are worked out on the important issues should the parties schedule the candlelight dinner. Even if there is no common ground and the differences in the issues are too great, go out to dinner anyway. Just discuss something else, and realize that a long-term intimate relationship probably isn't in the cards. Many people who have gone through the painful process of divorce may envy those who have learned the lesson earlier in the relationship: an old culture orientation does not mix well with a transitional one.

Increasing the awareness of the differences in social orientations is the major objective of the checklist. Don't ignore the warning signs of conflict of social characteristics in a prospective mate. Don't go on with life pretending the warning signals do not exist. Recognize that the differences lead each individual in a different direction and most likely will cause a parting of the ways. Differences in social orientation cannot be reconciled, so the sooner this is recognized the better for the future of both individuals.

Failure to receive a verbal response on a returned checklist or refusal to participate in part or completely is the same as silence, the old culture answer. In fact, silence is the tacit acknowledgement that the questions have exposed an old culture person who deliberately intends to keep his/her agenda hidden. Silence means that the other person has had insufficient time to develop a response to deflect the inquiry. Remember, silence is the same as the "Trust me" response.

Unless the parties have carefully identified issues to compromise on, and which ones are not, don't be induced into making compromises that will be regretted later. Human nature leads individuals, when under the heat of the moment, to do what is necessary to preserve the relationship. Unfortunately, such compromises are often in favor of the old culture image because human nature causes individuals to tend toward automatic responses, without thinking. In our culture, we are often told that opposites attract. Since there may be a lot of disagreement at first, we are told when things settle down everything will work itself out. Beware that a successful relationship of any duration is an illusion if the parties differ on fundamental issues. The reality is that while opposites often do attract, they do so for only a short time before reality sets in. If the parties do not share common interests and enjoy most things together, the chances for long-term success and happiness are remote. The concept that things will work themselves out really means that someone is going to yield to the desires of the other, sacrificing themselves, their goals, interests and personal feelings for the relationship.

Of course, staying together in a non-relationship is an option some individuals choose, willing to compromise and sacrifice personal goals and dreams for the sake of keeping the relationship together. Such an approach is strictly old culture. The greater the number of responses on the checklist that differ significantly, the more unlikely they will be resolved. The more frequently one confronts the old culture bias in an individual, the more that person will automatically lock into their images.

One of the areas often seen as superficial is called "brand wars." Brand wars exist where one person prefers using a certain brand of toothpaste, soap, mayonnaise or any one of a thousand other household items. The war begins when spouses differ on the choice of brand they will use when living together. The warning signs of a deeper problem arise when one person insists that the other adopt their preferred brand.

That person is not expressing their preference for the specific brand but their need to dominate and control the relationship, a strong old culture characteristic.

Notice that the rational solution of each selecting his or her preferred brand is not an acceptable option. The old culture person cannot accept separate brands because it means they must accept the other person on an equal basis. Because brand wars are not likely to surface until after the marriage ceremony, the checklist is often the only way to draw out such old culture thinking. A transitional person would not want to find out they are married to an old culture person months later when a brand war erupts, indicating different social orientations.

Ultimately, the only real choice where the internal images are not shared is avoidance. Putting distance between persons with opposing cultural characteristics is the only workable solution. Accepting others for who they are, not for personal objectives is the true solution for successful relationships.

Sometimes individuals delude themselves into thinking they have brought about a miraculous transformation in someone else, but what has really happened is that the other person has elected to become non-confrontational. The silent one has elected not to accept the other person for who they are. This process of delusion is often unconscious and usually takes place to maintain the relationship at any cost. As harsh as it appears, avoidance is the only way to protect oneself from strong, differing social characteristics. Happiness in the old culture is a mirage. At some time or another, those who embrace it will have to face reality. Usually the longer they delay, the more difficult facing reality will be.

Human beings have a natural human tendency to recoil from a non-emotional, rational approach to human relationships. Such a reaction is normal. Statistical figures tell us that a large number of marriages will not last and many that do are old culture ones maintained for the sake of the marriage.

Increasing the amount of money spent on the wedding ceremony will have no affect on the chances of success of the marriage. On the other hand, the checklist has a much better chance of promoting a successful long-term relationship than pouring money into a ceremony. The checklist simply deals with the reality of living together instead of reinforcing and dwelling on the old culture images.

The checklist included in this chapter is presented only as a guide. Work on developing a more detailed list for specific personal and financial circumstances. The checklist included is simply an attempt to provide a reality check into an emotionally charged situation. Marriages often take place based on emotional feelings, but they survive only by facing real issues successfully. If the checklist does nothing more than increase awareness of the differences in social and cultural orientation and the impact this has on human relationships, it will have served its purpose.

CHAPTER SEVENTEEN: NEW CULTURE DREAMS

The older single professional women are painfully aware that all is not rosy in the Transition. Chances are, when looking in the mirror, many have wondered just how transitional they actually are. In fact, someone may already have suggested to them that they need to take a little time off and consider having a personal life beyond a career. At a point in time, the older single professionals occasionally feel the tug of the biological clock and the power of the underlying old culture bias smoldering within their psyche. Suddenly, the older, single professional may ask, where is the husband or wife, family life and the castle? In fact, old culture associates and relatives may begin hinting that the single life style is negligent in fulfilling the societal obligation to make poor Adam whole again. To the old culture associates, relatives and friends are nagging that not living life according to the rules is scandalous.

A little anxiety for the targeted single person is perfectly normal. Unless they are conscious of the nature of the internal struggle, these feelings can be powerfully dangerous. However, hiding from reality is not possible. Arranging a night out with a few friends is fine, going to a nightclub, or the neighborhood sports bar. Just be prepared that the men and women there will be younger. Of course, this observation is minor compared to the fact the males there are most likely going to be strictly old culture in their social orientation. Most people never realized the existence of the differences in social orientation. So, now armed with awareness, it will be easier to recognize the old culture males. The simple question arises:

Where are the transitional men?

The whole experience will be a bit disconcerting at first, but knowing enough to ask the right questions will save a lot of misery. No one needs to follow what old culture people recommend. The answer, of course, is that our old friend culture is the culprit behind the anxiety and discomfort felt from the comments of friends, relatives and associates. The first thing for a single professional woman to remember is that it is highly unlikely to find a transitional male in a single's bar or nightclub.

Years ago, young women fell in love with their favorite rock star or Hollywood actor. Now, when they are older, reality descends and real relationships develop between people who meet in the course of their lives. Usually they "fall in love" with someone they actually meet and spend time with. This means adults can control their mate selection by spending time with people who have common interests and share the same social orientation.

During high school and college days, there were roughly an equal number of males and females. Sitting on a bar stool, looking around at all the strange faces, the single person might wonder what happened to all the poor Adams they knew back in school. The first thing to remember is that women led the social revolution due to economic pressures. When they did so, they left their male peers behind, absorbed in their old culture ways. As a society, we cannot expect men to make a quantum leap and catch up overnight. The cultural brainwashing is too deeply ingrained. When men began to realize their wives and girlfriends were going to earn as much money or more than they were, their cultural orientation froze. Some even lashed back in anger against their mate, rather than the real culprit, culture. To grow and survive, men need to learn how to deal with the conflict of the internal cultural image of the knight in shining armor and the fact that the world has changed, leaving the knight in shining armor in the graveyard. This change will only occur on a slow, incremental step-by-step basis. As a society, we need not worry; men will eventually catch up. For the human species to survive, this change is absolutely necessary. In the meantime, life goes on, and waiting for this to happen is pointless.

There's another reason transitional males are not found in the bar. The transitional male can detect a husband-hunter a mile away. They have already gone out of their way to avoid the husband-hunter; the husband hunter is an old culture female. Just as the transitional female is turned off by the approach of an old culture male, so too is the transitional male turned off by the old culture female looking for an old culture husband. One young woman expressed a common frustration:

I want to marry a man who is transitional.

Her statement points out her confusion. If she is old culture and husband hunting, there are old culture males readily available, and sports bars are as good as any place to find them. The men will be divorced, or at least claim they are. She won't have too much trouble finding one. On the other hand, if she is looking for a long-term relationship with a transitional male, she will have to develop interests in things beyond herself, which she can't do sitting in a sports bar. Only through shared common interests can long-term relationships evolve between transitional men and women.

A transitional person may or may not find the perfect marriage, but they have no interest in marriage unless they have the right relationship with their partner. The transitional individual's focus is on a meaningful relationship based on common interests and values. Marriage and family naturally flow out of a solid relationship, but they are not objectives in and of themselves. This point is a very important difference from old culture thinking and has already shown up in the population composition of our society. The old concept of the biological family represented by the husband, wife and biological children has drastically dropped as a percentage of total households. Instead of allowing the old culture bias within determine the future based on the concepts of the past, individuals now are developing a wide range of interests and activities beyond the self.

No matter what one's marital status is, life can only be lived to its fullest through meaningful involvement in broad areas of interests. When the old culture concept of family keeps nagging at the individual, some have answered this tug of nature and culture by adopting a child. Today, many individuals have done so, without a marriage partner. Instead of worrying about biological or societal limitations, individuals can direct this energy toward helping the problems of other human beings. All over the world, thousands of orphaned children die each day because there is no one to care for them. The modern family is different from the one of the American Dark Ages. The current new wave of adoption of orphans from foreign countries is playing a key role in forging a new definition of family. For example:

> *I never thought I would find myself divorced and living alone. Yet, at the same time, I have a successful career. I felt that my life was not complete until the day I adopted my daughter. I never thought I could be so happy.*

While thinking about the possibility of a family, one must think too about what marriage means to them. Certainly, the possibility exists that one may find someone special because more men are catching up with the Revolution and are becoming transitional every day. However, be forewarned that marriage, too, is changing. Gradually, the old culture concept of marriage may fade away like the old image of the castle where the mighty white steed has withered away and died.

Many couples are forging new ways to celebrate a new concept of the wedding ceremony and marriage. Since the future continually evolves in its own way and at its own pace, no one can predict what the culture of the future will really be like as we travel on the journey through the Transition. The news media enthusiastically reports some of the new ways couples are celebrating marriage. Occasionally we hear of couples that have begun their new relationship by bungi-jumping off bridges or even diving out of airplanes in parachutes, brazenly sky diving into their new future together. One couple took a new, casual approach by exchanging their vows to each other on the evening of Friday the Thirteenth, under the light of the full moon. Guests were discouraged from bringing gifts but encouraged to dress casually and bring covered dishes to share after the ceremony. The groom had gifted the bride with a hand-hewn, wooden swing, which they installed in the front yard to optimize their view of the full moon. Guests brought umbrellas, which, in fun, were superstitiously lined up along the front porch in a colorful array to ward off any potential rain showers. As the minister arrived to officiate the ceremony, which the bride and groom had written, he noted a huge contrail over the top of the rising full moon in the shape of an enormous cross. The weather remained rain-free. The couple exchanged their personally composed vows to each other with their close friends and relatives, witnessing the event in the bride's front yard. Certainly this celebration is one that has broken most of the traditional trappings of wedding customs. A celebration such as this one is very meaningful to the participants and a very practical approach to the changing customs in this country, and a practical, reflection of the courage of couples to forge new ways to express their commitment to each other. Setting such an example only affords others the courage to follow suit and explore what has meaning for them.

As our society and culture evolve and new images and standards emerge, more and more individuals will find the courage and creativity to develop what they see as an expression of their relationship. With the tremendous expenses generally incurred in a traditional wedding ceremony and the frequent failure of relationships, the matter of marriage and wedding ceremonies is changing and will continue to evolve. These are times where, at least in the United States, couples with vastly differing cultures are finding ways to blend these differences into a new way that works for them and their families. The dream of the White Knight is fading fast into a memory and a new, exciting reality is emerging with each couple as they forge new ground in their relationships and ways to celebrate the beginning of a lifetime commitment. Who knows where the Transition will take our culture. As with all revolutions, this Transition is not without its drawbacks and hurdles. The evidence of social and political backlash is expressed everyday on television and in the media. We see, with the current wave of reality television shows, contestants who compete with 20-30 others for a chance at a desired potential spouse in Prince Millibucks Charming, shows with video cameras documenting the daily life of some famous celebrity or sports figure, and a plethora of makeover shows where the candidate experiences a new wardrobe, new make up, new hairdo, and even body-reshaping plastic surgery to fit their "dream." Generally, national politicians are refusing to acknowledge the death throws of the traditional two-parent, two biological child family. Slowly various movements on the state level are recognizing the true make up of the current cultural family – most are non-traditional in composition with siblings, friends and relatives sharing living accommodations. These new family relationships are real, practical for raising young children in a multi-generational family and rising to fill the needs for taking care of the handicapped and elderly. Many of these changes are permanent as a result of the revolution, the women's movement, rising cost of living and other personal and political factors.

Our culture is gradually becoming global, extending influences into the third world countries where Disney theme parks and McDonald's golden arches are appearing in traditionally vegetarian, closed cast societies. Where we will end up globally will take longer to develop than the changes we have experienced here in the United States. Worldwide effects of the Revolution and Transition are inevitable.

If more and more couples are recognizing each partner as an individual who can stand alone as well as participate in the marriage relationship, where does that leave the children? If more women begin to retain their birth names, how will the new Transitional couples name their children? Some have selected names that have no reference to either of the parents. Most still recognize our cultural traditions of the male family lineage. Where all this will this end up is anyone's projection, one as good as the next. The future bodes to be filled with unpredictable changes due to cultural changes and increasing natural disasters playing significant roles in family composition and location. Each individual continues to be defined by their personal internal images as each individual experiences their own internal video camera and an individual interpretation of their personal dream. The future is wide open for possibilities which hopefully will include settling the "battle or war of the sexes" and narrowing the great divide so that a new understanding emerges for the betterment of each individual, society and most importantly, the children. Of course, the children are the most important because they **are** the future.

CHAPTER EIGHTEEN: LIVING TODAY

An observant young woman asked:

Why is it that fifty people attended my marriage ceremony, but not one of them showed up to support me when I went through my divorce, the one time I needed my friends the most?

Since the wedding ceremony is simply a reaffirmation of the old culture images for all who attend, perhaps the guests might wonder if they attended as much for themselves as for the bride and groom. Is the reality of living today so far from the old culture images that people need an occasional boost to reinforce their internal perceptions of themselves? Occasionally, everyone has the opportunity to attend a wedding ceremony. Often the ceremonies are virtually identical with minor touches expressed by the personalities involved. Is this conformity evidence of the power of the old culture images to control us as individuals? A middle-aged woman shared her perspective in the following comment:

I remember saying, "I do." Now, years later, I wonder exactly what it was that I agreed to do. Whatever it was, it certainly wasn't what he thought I agreed to do, that's for sure. In any case, whatever I agreed to do back then, I'm sure I wouldn't agree to do it today.

The first young woman going through her divorce would agree. Guests flock to the wedding ceremony, but they certainly are nowhere to be seen when divorce moves in. In fact, the courtroom is empty except for the attorneys and the judge. In some cases, even the participants are absent, sending the attorney in to handle the whole unpleasant affair. Does culture really explain why those who attend the wedding are absent when the relationship crumbles into a divorce action? Could it be that divorce is such a threat to the old culture images that people disappear at the very mention of the word?

The second woman's point was that people seldom understand what they mean even when they go through the ceremony and say the words. How many times has the bride said her wedding seemed to be a dream and can't possibly be real? Why is it that no one dares to tell her she might be right? One woman's observation illustrates the issue:

> *Most brides believe their wedding day is the greatest day in their lives. Many call it a day when they are "queen for a day." It is really not her day; they are just being duped into believing the myth. It's not her day; it's really his day. The bride gives up everything, her name and even her identity while he gets a lifetime servant. In the majority of cases, she becomes the homemaker, cooking, cleaning and doing the laundry and grocery shopping while he is relieved of doing these tasks for himself. She must now do these tasks for him, any children and for herself. The bride is so distracted by planning the details of the ceremony. She doesn't take the time to notice what is really happening to her. Could it be that she is right? Is celebration of the wedding ceremony nothing more than a celebration of the merger of the female back into the male as a confirmation of the old fable and nothing more? Does society still fail to recognize the individuals involved and how unique they are? Has our culture tainted our perspective enough to ignored the issues so necessary to develop a lasting relationship for the sake of a ceremony?*

If the only glue holding a marriage together as time passes is the album of posed photographs, the present divorce rate may be more easily understood. One woman's observation comes to mind:

> *Why is it that the most important person at the wedding seems to be the photographer? Why is there so much emphasis on taking pictures? Shouldn't a wedding be a completely spontaneous event? Why is it so carefully choreographed and practiced? Why are there so many posed photographs? I thought I was shooting a commercial instead of getting married. I got in and out of the*

carriage three times, just so the photographer could get a perfect picture. To me, it seemed like we were all dressed up in costumes. No one was comfortable in the formal attire and will never wear it again. To me, the cake and the carriage seemed to be just fancy props in a television commercial.

Could the wedding ceremony actually be the commercial for the tradition itself, more than for the participants? How many times does the bride or groom ever look at those pictures over the years? One story that dramatically illustrates the issue that people do not know what marriage means when they go through the ceremony was told by a man, not a woman:

We were married only six months when she told me the news that she was pregnant. That day was the most traumatic day of my life. I will never forget it. I was excited that I was going to be a father, but she also told me something else. She informed me that sex is for making babies so now that she was pregnant, that was the end of sex. At the time, I remember thinking she was joking, but I soon discovered I was wrong.

The middle-aged woman's story of not knowing what it was that she agreed to do on her wedding day is dramatically reinforced by the above example. Only this time the tide is turned against the male. Culture affects more of human behavior than most participants willingly admit. The power of culture over the relationship called marriage has the greatest influence on personal lives. As long as people act automatically, going through the ceremony without thinking about what it means, our lives will remain mired in the old traditions of the past. As the marriage partners travel down the road of life, they discover that what they expected is far different than what they got. The statistics on divorce continue to remind us that what we are doing is not relevant to the world in which we live.

Living today requires acknowledgement that the enemy we face daily in our lives is our culture. Only then can we hope to find a way to update the practices we have kept alive from the days back on the farm. A common comment illustrates the point:

My wedding was beautiful. In fact, everything was perfect. It was exactly what I wanted, but I never looked beyond the ceremony. Six months later I realized the real world of living together had nothing to do with the ceremony.

The success of real estate closings lies in the details. Using this model as a guide may help us update the concept of marriage to be more relevant today. The success of a real estate transaction depends on the lack of surprise at the closing table. This means that every detail, no matter how great or small, is provided in a written document. Any differences or misunderstandings are negotiated and spelled out in writing signed by all the parties. There are no surprises at the closing table. Negotiation of all the details of the transaction up front results in disclosure specifically designed to avoid surprises. This mode of operating makes the real estate contract a good model for a solution to the difficulties our culture is now having with marriage. Why not address every issue in advance and put the agreement in writing? Such an idea is not an attempt to start a new revolution but is a reaction to the one we have just gone through. Many wealthy people including royalty and Hollywood stars have been doing this for years with prenuptial agreements. A very small percentage of real estate transactions wind up in court as a result. As long as individuals enter into the most important personal relationship of their lives automatically, without thought and without a clear agreement on the terms, the ever increasing complexity of our lives assures that marriages will continue to fail at the alarming rate we see now.

Every person is unique and comes to the wedding ceremony with differing personal and financial backgrounds. These facts require flexibility not rigid ritualistic compliance to behavior norms dating back to the formation of our country. A modernization of marriage based on the reality of the world of today will go a long way to reduce the divorce rate, and guide us to more rewarding personal and family lives. Personal relationships are simply too important to leave to chance, drink a glass of champagne in celebration, and hope for the best.

Hopefully the future will take us to a new place in forging successful partnering relationships in the face of the ever-increasing number of divorces. Perhaps structuring the institution of marriage around an extensive written agreement would help answer the problem. Such a document would not just be based on the issues raised in our checklist, but would be structured around unique needs and desires of the prospective partners. Of course, such an agreement would only be successful if every issue, including such sensitive topics as sex, infidelity, children, in-laws, relatives and property rights are carefully and honestly spelled out. If the negotiation process breaks down and what appeared to be a promising relationship dissolves such that poor Adam won't be made whole, so be it. In such a world, at least divorce may dwindle down to insignificance, and marriage will have a better chance of being an agreement for life between equal human beings.

Learning about personal relations requires reading a good book on the subject. Why should this be any different than real estate? To participate in real estate transactions, most people wisely seek the advice and assistance of an attorney, accountant or financial advisor for the most valuable asset they will purchase. Why not do the same for the most important relationship in our lives? Perhaps most people have placed their heads in the sand, not recognizing that marriage is not personal relationship, but a legal one. This fact is brought home with electrifying effects when the relationship dissolves. Don't most people seek the advise of an investment or financial advisor for making long term investments? Why not do the same when selecting a life partner?

One's personal ability to survive in today's world also requires heightened awareness of the influence of culture over decision-making. Failure to recognize the important issues in life in time to stop and ask questions will result in failure to prevent long-term problems before it is too late. No self-help book in the world will solve a situation out of control. The common thread in every chapter in this book is the custom called marriage. The one most important issue in marriage is what marriage means to the individuals planning to join together for life. The answer to that question is not in any book, but must come from inside the parties involved. By now the solution will depend on whether the participants are knowledgeable of each other's social orientation: whether old culture or transitional, and to what degree and on what issues. The extent to which one believes marriage is the merger of the female back into the male, and the degree to which one retains the old fables as part of one's belief system, is the real issue between the parties. One young woman clearly expressed her personal conflict with the old culture:

> *I first realized I had changed when I went to try on my wedding dress. For some reason I felt a bit awkward and ill at ease. I wondered what my fiancé would say if he knew how I felt.*

The underlying issue in her comment is whether a transitional woman should wear a traditional wedding dress when she gets married. The answer is that she must do what is right for her as an individual. Since she is transitional, it is likely her fiancé is also transitional, in which case there is no reason to worry about what he thinks. A transitional male doesn't care what kind of ceremony she elects. His only interest will be her happiness and well being no matter what the day. Thus, the question of what to wear on her wedding day is hers and hers alone. All of us living today are creatures of our culture, and the traditional old culture wedding ceremony is part of who we are. Deep in the subconscious, every transitional person still carries the remnants of the old culture images, so if the wedding dress and a conventional ceremony are what she wants, she should not hesitate to make the arrangements. If there is another alternative, that is a possibility also. By now the bride should be able to separate marriage from its symbols for what should be a once in a lifetime event. Everything the couple can do to reinforce and build on the relationship is important. Ideally, a conventional ceremony that strengthens the relationship is so much the better when it has true meaning for both individuals joining together as a couple.

The most important issue to realize is that the force that holds individuals back from living life to its fullest potential does not reside in others, but within the self. Individuals who develop a simple awareness that old habits, customs and traditions can trap them personally and financially are on the way to living a full and rewarding life in the Transition. One's knowledge of the power of culture on decision-making and on the degree to which one will allow this power to control the important issues in life is the key to growing to achieve one's greatest potential.

EPILOGUE

At the end of the television show, all the contestants have been reduced from twenty-five down to the final winner. The reality show ends with an elaborate wedding of Prince Millibucks Charming to the blissful Pauper Princess. Outside, eager friends, guests, and well-wishers line up on both sides of the steps leading down from the chapel to the limousine waiting at the curb.
"Here they come, Peter Prince Charming and Penelope Princess Charming, his wife," says a young woman speaking to an older lady standing next to her.
"Yes, his wife and personal possession," responds the older lady cynically, as she smiles and turns to face the younger woman.
"Just think. Now they are one," answers the younger woman, ignoring the wise old lady's comment.
 "Do you think that means he plans to add her name on the deed to the castle?" inquires the older woman cynically, as the happy couple appears on the landing at the top of the stairs.
"I don't know," replies the younger woman, taken aback by the question, as the newly weds start down the steps.
"I wonder what *she* thinks he's going to do?" inquires the older woman, pressing the issue as the newly weds pass by.
"You can't ask *that* kind of question, now."
"Why not? It's certainly valid *now*."
"This isn't the time. You might destroy the dream," answers the younger woman, showing a little annoyance at the older woman's inquiry, as the couple descends the last few steps to the limousine.
"If we can't ask that question now, someone is wasting a lot of money,

and this celebration is just an illusion," observes the older woman. "Perhaps, but reality can wait. Right now, this is a wonderful celebration of merger. It's a special day for all of us," responds the younger woman happily, waiving as the limousine pulls away.

"What about you, young lady? Someday it will be your turn."

"Me? Goodness no. I'm divorced."

ABOUT THE AUTHORS

Jon C. Hall graduated from Purdue University, Lafayette, Indiana, and Indiana University School of Law-Indianapolis. He was admitted to the Indiana Bar, the Illinois Bar, and the Florida Bar.

He worked many years in the field of real estate law in Indiana, Illinois and Florida. Due to health reasons, he retired from the active practice of law in 2000. During his retirement years he taught law course to paralegals at Essex County Community college in New Jersey where he lived with his sister until his death in 2004. He maintained an active interest in nature and environmental issues, and archaeology. He is a former member of the South Florida Archaeological Association, the Florida Anthropological Society and the Roebling Chapter of the National Society for Industrial Archaeology.

Jon expanded his natural gift for writing and story telling while recuperating from health adversities. He was active in The Write Group in Montclair, New Jersey contributing a wealth of professionalism toward the success of the group.

****

Barbara D. Hall graduated from Wittenberg University in Springfield, Ohio and obtained a master's degree from The Ohio State University in Columbus, Ohio.

She worked many years in the pharmaceutical industry specializing in Food and Drug Law. In addition, she maintains a New Jersey Real Estate License; investing and managing real estate properties. In retirement, she assisted her brother during the last few years of his life writing and editing books, sharing many interests including photography, traveling, nature, archaeology and eating blueberries.

Barbara is a member of The Write Group in Montclair, New Jersey and the International Women's Writing Guild.

OTHER PUBLICATIONS

BOKURU, by Jon C. Hall, edited by Barbara D. Hall, AuthorHouse, Bloomington, Indiana, published June 2005.

Visit our website at: www.ournaturematters.net

Printed in the United States
202638BV00003B/22-48/A